Bison

Animal
Series editor: Jonathan Burt

Already published

Albatross Graham Barwell · *Ant* Charlotte Sleigh · *Ape* John Sorenson · *Badger* Daniel Heath Justice
Bear Robert E. Bieder · *Bee* Claire Preston · *Beaver* Rachel Poliquin · *Bison* Desmond Morris
Camel Robert Irwin · *Cat* Katharine M. Rogers · *Chicken* Annie Potts · *Cockroach* Marion Copeland
Cow Hannah Velten · *Crocodile* Dan Wylie · *Crow* Boria Sax · *Deer* John Fletcher · *Dog* Susan McHugh
Dolphin Alan Rauch · *Donkey* Jill Bough · *Duck* Victoria de Rijke · *Eagle* Janine Rogers
Eel Richard Schweid · *Elephant* Dan Wylie · *Falcon* Helen Macdonald · *Flamingo* Caitlin R. Kight
Fly Steven Connor · *Fox* Martin Wallen · *Frog* Charlotte Sleigh · *Giraffe* Edgar Williams
Goat Joy Hinson · *Gorilla* Ted Gott and Kathryn Weir · *Guinea Pig* Dorothy Yamamoto
Hare Simon Carnell · *Hedgehog* Hugh Warwick · *Horse* Elaine Walker · *Hyena* Mikita Brottman
Kangaroo John Simons · *Leech* Robert G. W. Kirk and Neil Pemberton · *Leopard* Desmond Morris
Lion Deirdre Jackson · *Lobster* Richard J. King · *Monkey* Desmond Morris · *Moose* Kevin Jackson
Mosquito Richard Jones · *Mouse* Georgie Carroll · *Octopus* Richard Schweid · *Ostrich* Edgar Williams
Otter Daniel Allen · *Owl* Desmond Morris · *Oyster* Rebecca Stott · *Parrot* Paul Carter
Peacock Christine E. Jackson · *Penguin* Stephen Martin · *Pig* Brett Mizelle · *Pigeon* Barbara Allen
Rabbit Victoria Dickenson · *Rat* Jonathan Burt · *Rhinoceros* Kelly Enright · *Salmon* Peter Coates
Shark Dean Crawford · *Snail* Peter Williams · *Snake* Drake Stutesman · *Sparrow* Kim Todd
Spider Katarzyna and Sergiusz Michalski · *Swan* Peter Young · *Tiger* Susie Green · *Tortoise* Peter Young
Trout James Owen · *Vulture* Thom van Dooren · *Walrus* John Miller and Louise Miller · *Whale* Joe Roman
Wolf Garry Marvin

Bison

Desmond Morris

REAKTION BOOKS

Published by
REAKTION BOOKS LTD
Unit 32, Waterside
44–48 Wharf Road
London N1 7UX, UK
www.reaktionbooks.co.uk

First published 2015
Copyright © Desmond Morris 2015

Printed in India by Replika Press Pvt. Ltd.

A catalogue record for this book is available from the British Library

ISBN 978 1 78023 424 3

Contents

Introduction

The mighty bison was an evolutionary triumph. Its huge frame, great hump, massive chest, thick neck and sharp horns combined to make it almost invincible. Even the most savage predator would think twice before tackling a healthy adult bison. And any attack on a young one would be met with a furious defence by an angry parent. Only the old and the sick would fall easily to a predator's assault.

As a result, the bison herds grew and grew until there were countless millions of these magnificent animals occupying the woodlands and grasslands of Europe, northern Asia and North America. It was a shining star in the evolutionary story of the hoofed mammals. Then it all went wrong. A new predator arrived on the scene, a bipedal primate with a big brain that was clever enough to fashion artificial weapons – spears, axes and arrows – with which it could assail the bison's mountain of flesh. Worse still, this new killer's brain was sharp enough to devise cunning traps and strategies, such as driving stampeding herds over clifftops, giving the hunters a significant advantage over the previously invincible giants.

Worse still was to come. When primitive weapons were replaced by modern ones, the golden age of the bison was over. When humans invented firearms, the glory days of the great ungulate were numbered. In less than a century, the vast herds

Bison in river, Yellowstone National Park, 1994.

were nearly slaughtered into extinction. Eventually the countless millions dwindled to literally a few hundred animals. Happily, on the very verge of extinction, these last, pathetic remnants were saved for posterity by the actions of a few caring individuals who protected them and encouraged them to start breeding again. Today, their numbers have started rising and they are safe from dying out, although they will never again roam the great open spaces in their millions, because most of those spaces are now filled with farms, towns and roads. The human predator has won the day and spread over the land surface of the planet with a global dominance the like of which has not been seen since the age of the dinosaurs. Now, other large mammals are only allowed to thrive courtesy of the planet's new, human masters. In their wild state they have become increasingly rare. Only those that succumbed to domestication have increased in number. A close relative of the bison, the aurochs, the wild ancestor of domestic cattle, may no longer exist in its natural state, but there are well over one billion animals of this species living in captivity, as subdued servants of the great human predator. In the process, they have lost a great deal of their original, wild character. Their colours and shapes have been changed to suit human preferences, or commercial considerations, and they have been selectively bred for docility and milk production.

The proud bison has never had to suffer these indignities, but it has not escaped entirely. Since its recovery, its numbers have increased so dramatically in the twenty-first century that some of the herds are now being managed for meat production. And because of ever-increasing human populations, even the herds that are being maintained for conservation purposes have to be managed in restricted areas. However, although its existence

Bison and calf, Yellowstone National Park, 2013.

today, like that of the downtrodden domestic cattle, must be subject to human control, it has, at least, managed to retain its wild appearance and its stubbornly aggressive personality, and it is still allowed, in most places, to run in its natural herds.

So, this book is a story of a splendid beast that suffered a mass slaughter at the hands of a ferocious predator who, at the very last moment, saw the error of his ways and saved his victim from final annihilation. We can never give the bison back its triumphant past, but with our new, more respectful attitude towards our wild animal companions, its future seems assured, even if it has to be a limited existence, relying on parks, reserves and sanctuaries. The iconic bison deserves no less.

CONFUSION OVER NAMES: BISON AND BUFFALO

There has been some confusion over the names 'bison' and 'buffalo'. 'Bison' derives from Latin and by the fourteenth century was in use to describe the European bison. When its American relative was discovered, its close similarity led, inevitably, to it being called the American bison and this remains its official title. However, in the seventeenth century it also acquired the popular name of 'buffalo', probably from French trappers who were by now scouring the New World for animal hides.

Unfortunately, the name 'buffalo' had already been given to the Cape buffalo of Africa and the water buffalo of India, neither of which was closely related to the European bison. Because of this prior use for these other species, scientists were opposed to the use of the name buffalo for the American species as well and in the eighteenth century one authority formally complained: 'This animal has generally been called the buffalo but very improperly.'

Despite scientific disapproval, however, the popularity of the name 'buffalo' in America was such that, by the nineteenth century, it had been widely accepted by the general public there. The arrival on the scene of the infamous Buffalo Bill helped this cause, but scientists still resisted it and, even today, the term American bison is always used by serious students of the species.

Further confusion exists over names because the European bison also has an alternative name. From early days, the name 'wisent' has been applied to the European species. This has a Teutonic or German root, coming from the early 'wisand' or 'wisund'. It is still met with in the literature, but has never ousted the official name of European bison.

To sum up, 'bison' and 'buffalo' have the following modern usage:

OFFICIAL NAME	ALTERNATIVE NAME	SCIENTIFIC NAME
European bison	Wisent	*Bos bonasus*
American bison	American buffalo	*Bos bos*
African buffalo	Cape buffalo	*Synceros caffer*
Water buffalo	Indian or Asiatic buffalo	*Bubalis bubalis*

THE TWO SPECIES OF BISON

The two forms of bison living today, the European and the American, are so similar that some authorities believe they should be considered as a single species. There are, however, a number of minor differences that suggest this view is mistaken. These differences are as follows:

- The European bison has fifteen pairs of ribs; the American bison has only fourteen
- The European has five lumbar vertebrae; the American has only four
- The European has a slimmer build than the American

- The European weighs slightly less on average than the American
- The European has longer legs than the American
- The European is taller at the shoulder than the American
- The European has shorter hair on its forequarters, head and neck than the American
- The European has a longer tail than the American
- The European prefers to lock horns when fighting; the American prefers to headbutt.

Because these differences, although significant, are so small, in some sections of this book the bison is treated as a single entity. However, when the European and American histories of these animals are being discussed, it makes more sense to treat them separately.

1 Prehistoric Bison

The great flowering of art that occurred on the walls of caves in Western Europe between 30,000 and 10,000 years ago was essentially a celebration of the animal prey of our early human ancestors. Interestingly, they did not honour their smaller prey with commemorative portraits on their cave walls, even when these smaller creatures were making up the bulk of their diet. Instead, in their art, they focused on their larger, more impressive quarry. This inevitably led to depictions of bison, along with rhinoceros, mammoth, horse, deer and aurochs.

Bison appear on the walls of many of the decorated caves in France and northern Spain, but their popularity varies from cave to cave. On the famous ceiling of the Altamira cave in northern Spain, the bison is by far the most common subject in the great panel of animals. The percentages are as follows: bison 77 per cent; wild boar 14 per cent; horse 4.5 per cent; deer 4.5 per cent.

In another famous cave, Lascaux, the figures are very different. There, the horse accounts for 60 per cent, deer for 14 per cent, while the bison accounts for only 4 per cent. This difference means one of two things. Either the bison were more common in northern Spain than they were in central France, or there was a difference in their value to the two hunting groups. The Altamira tribe may have seen themselves primarily as bison-hunters, while

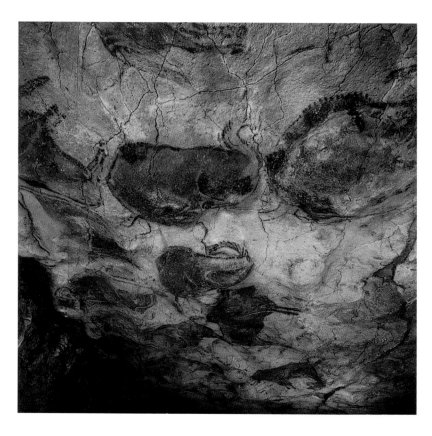

Bison on the roof of the Altamira cave, Spain.

the Lascaux tribe may have looked upon themselves as the great equine specialists.

The most astonishing feature of these very early human works of art is that they are so skilful. With most ancient and tribal art there are exaggerations and simplifications in the animal images that are created. Details are omitted and shapes become schematic. Where animals become emblems they are often little more than a characteristic squiggle. A blob with forked lines coming out of the top is enough to capture the essence of a deer and its antlers. A vertical, two-legged blob becomes a human. No more is needed. But the ancient cave artists rejected the use of such simple pictograms. Almost alone among ancient artists they set out to make accurate portrayals of their animals, with naturalistic proportions and precise details.

From this we can conclude that their lovingly created bison paintings did not function as emblems or symbols. They were, instead, precise renderings of particular, individual animals. They were, in other words, commemorative portraits and this is why they had to be so accurate. Supporting this interpretation is the fact that they were all clearly portrayed in postures of death. These were not living bison, they were freshly slain bison. The only way that these artists could have been so anatomically correct in their work was if they had gone to the site of one of their great kills – a huge triumph bearing in mind their primitive weapons – and made a charcoal drawing on a piece of dried animal pelt. Taking

Two bison bulls at the Lascaux cave in central France; the one on the left is shedding its winter fur.

One of the Altamira bison in a curled-up posture of death.

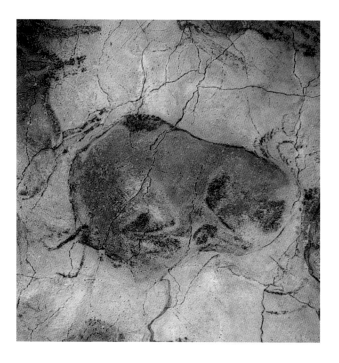

this to the cave and lighting an oil lamp, they could then set about copying the drawing onto the wall with coloured pigments, such as red and brown ochres. We have no proof that this happened, of course, but it is hard to see how they could be so accurate without this visual aid.

One of the most remarkable details of the cave paintings is that the bison and the other large ungulates are all shown with their feet apparently dangling in the air. The angle of the hooves, in all cases, shows that there are not weight-bearing. In other words, although the animals look to us as if they are standing up, they are in reality being portrayed lying down. Again, this supports the idea that they are all dead and were sketched where they fell.

An Australian artist, Percy Leason, took the trouble to visit a slaughterhouse and photograph the legs of animals before and after they were killed, and his photographs confirm that the 'dangling' feet of the cave paintings are those of freshly dead animals.[1]

With a few of the bison paintings there can be no doubt about their condition. In a famous one at the Lascaux cave the subject actually has its entrails hanging out, and several of the Altamira ones are curled up in awkward postures not seen in life. Still others are shown with arrows or spears sticking into their bodies. A unique feature of the Lascaux 'entrail bison' is that the body of a dead human hunter lies alongside it. The implication is that this particular bison killed the hunter before it was itself slain and that the artist extended his commemoration of the animal to include this event. The human figure has been given all kinds of imaginative interpretations. It has been described as ithyphallic

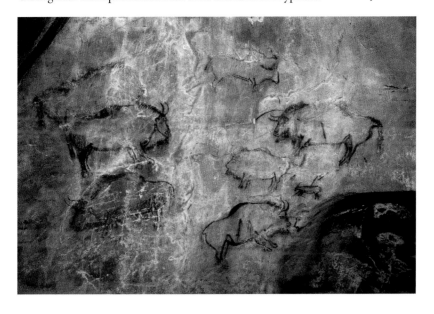

Panel of five bison on the wall of the Niaux cave, Ariège, France, showing remarkable anatomical accuracy.

and bird-headed and given the magical role of 'conductor of souls'. In other words, it has been elevated to the level of a supernatural being, instead of merely a dead hunter, gored by a fatally injured bison. The sober truth is that it is neither ithyphallic nor bird-headed. The line that is interpreted as a phallus is not convincing. Its rough shape suggests that it is more likely to indicate the injury where the man was gored. The head is not that of a bird but of a human. The two lines that seem to give it a bird's beak are more sensibly seen as the man's hair protruding from the back of his head which is twisted to his right. Similar, stiff, firm lines are employed to represent the hair of the bison.

The bison itself has also been endowed with special qualities. Writing in 1952, the famous cave specialist the Abbé Breuil described the bison as angry and threatening the man, with its tail lashing the air in fury.[2] He had overlooked the fact that the

A Lascaux bison with its entrails hanging out and a spear resting on its body.

hooves are pointing downwards and are not weight-bearing, demonstrating that the animal is lying on its side next to the fallen hunter and that both are dead. Surprisingly this interpretation of the cave paintings as representing carcasses is not usually stressed in books about the ancient artists. It is as if the authors feel it will somehow reduce the dramatic impact of Palaeolithic art to describe the images as commemorative portraits of dead animals. But this seems to be the only explanation that makes any sense.

It is perhaps worth pointing out that, even today, a big game hunter cannot resist having his photograph taken standing, grinning, over his kill. The moment of triumph has to be recorded. He would not do this with a dead rabbit, but he would insist on it if he had just shot a large, dangerous animal. So it was with the ancient hunters who, having no cameras, had to paint their greatest kills to enshrine the memories of their most spectacular hunting victories. This interpretation also explains why there are no compositions on the cave walls. Each animal portrait is a separate entity. It may be close to other animals but this is merely jumbled juxtaposition, not organized composition. Indeed, in many cases, one artist has brusquely over-painted, or partially obscured, the work of another. His own, personal commemorative image is all that matters to him. The others are merely a nuisance, to be avoided if possible, but, if space is running out, to be covered.

There are several cases where claims have been made that this rule (accidental juxtaposition but no planned composition) has been broken. A famous one concerns a strange image in the deepest chamber of the Chauvet cave. This has been interpreted as a human female pubic triangle in close proximity to a bison. The chances are that this proximity is accidental, a case of two different artists using the same space, but some cave specialists have seen it as something much more complicated and significant. They see the

The human female reproductive organs, said to resemble the head and horns of a bison, thus making a bison a symbol of the primeval Goddess.

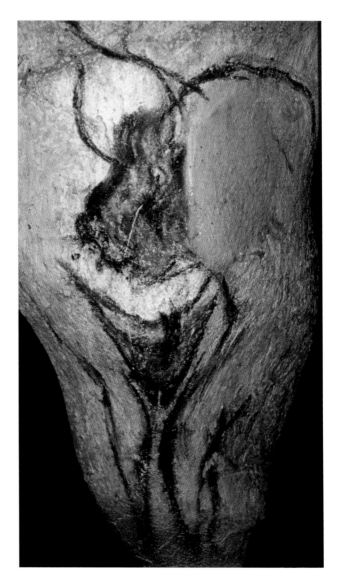

The unique, human female pubic triangle in the Chauvet cave, France, with a bison apparently hovering over it.

pubic triangle as part of a Venus figure and insist that the Venus and the 'sorcerer or man-bison' to its right have an intimate relationship that 'cannot be simply fortuitous'.[3] Some authors go even further and suggest that the head of the bison is the regenerating womb of the goddess. They see the positioning of the head of the Chauvet bison over the belly of the Venus as highly significant. Marija Gimbutas states that the importance of the bison in prehistoric cave art 'derives from the intimate relationship between the bison and the Goddess; the fact that the woman and the bison both have a pregnancy of nine months may help to account for this'.[4] She also refers to 'the extraordinary likeness of the female uterus and fallopian tubes to the head and horns of a bull'. Since there is no possible way to test these theories or to work out how a cave artist in the Old Stone Age would have gained knowledge about the reproductive significance, or the hornlike shape of fallopian tubes, it is best to discard them and see a bison on a cave wall simply as a bison.

Another over-imaginative interpretation has been conjured up for an image on the wall of the cave known as Les Trois Frères. It has been described as a sorcerer playing music to a bison, which turns its head to listen. A much simpler explanation is that the figure on the right is a human hunter dressed in the mask and hide of a bison, a disguise enabling him to get close to his victim. Similar images can be found in the Victorian paintings of American Indians stalking bison or performing bison dances. Furthermore, the bison is not turning its head. The head that appears to have been turned belongs to a different animal from the one whose body is facing away from the human figure. Once again, observers are too keen to interpret composed scenes on the cave walls when none are present.

One thing that is certainly clear from the wonderful cave art that has miraculously survived for so long is that ten or twenty

A reconstruction of the so-called 'sorcerer' in Les Trois Frères cave, Ariège, France, with bison.

thousand years ago, the bison was hugely important as a prey animal to our ancient ancestors. When even earlier ancestors left Africa and moved to the cooler regions of the north, the sudden absence of the familiar antelope and zebra did not bother them. In their place they found other victims for their slowly improving hunting skills. One of the most challenging of these must have been the great bison, with its delicious and plentiful meat. It may have been bigger and more dangerous, but the prize, when one was taken, would be outstanding.

CAVE SCULPTURE AND RELIEFS

In addition to the famous cave paintings, there are also several remarkable examples of three-dimensional bison created by the Palaeolithic artists. The most impressive is the pair of slain bison lying on the floor of Le Tuc d'Audoubert cave in the foothills of the Pyrenees in the south of France. Each animal is about 60 cm (2 ft) long and was fashioned from clay. Incisions were made to create the facial features and also the thick hair above and below the neck. The realistic proportions of the two beasts are skilfully achieved and the way that these two clay models have survived the passage of more than 12,000 years is amazing.

One prehistoric artist cunningly created three-dimensional paintings of bison. He did this by applying his paint to bulging rocks that had the rough shape of the animals. A close look at one of these, in the cave at Font-de-Gaume, reveals how well he managed to convey the heavy bulk of the bison's great lumbering, yet athletic, body. Also, the skilful way in which he handles the perspective when depicting the horns is incredible for an artist working around 17,000 BC. Other bison appear as reliefs on cave floors or as incised images on bones and antlers. Again, these show meticulous attention to realism and to natural proportions, without any of the exaggerations or simplifications found in most other forms of early or tribal art.

At the Niaux Cave in the Pyrenees, more than half a mile from the cave entrance, there is a wonderfully fashioned bison lying

Large clay models of two dead bison at Tuc d'Audoubert, Ariège, France.

on the floor. It was created by drawing with fingers in the soft mud and has miraculously remained there for more than 10,000 years. The artist has shown very clearly how the beast was slain, gouging three deep holes in the centre of its body to indicate the position of its wounds, and then adding an arrowhead or spear-head symbol to each to make it clear that the holes were made by hunters. It is no wonder that Picasso, when he was shown pictures of Palaeolithic cave art, snorted 'We have discovered nothing!'

One of the most exquisite bison images known from this early period is a small etching on a reindeer antler made about 14,000 years ago. It was found in the Dordogne region of central France and was originally called 'The Wounded Bison' because of its unusual posture, with the head twisted back against the chest. However, on closer inspection it is clear that, unlike the images on the walls of the prehistoric caves, this is not a dead bison, but

The brilliantly shaped bison at Font-de-Gaume in southwest France.

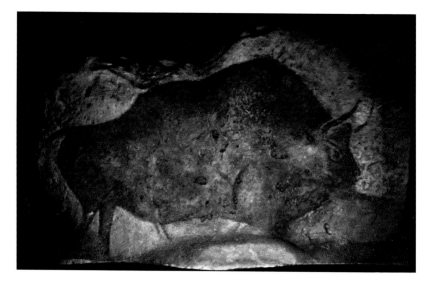

The Niaux bison, created by fingers on the floor of the cave.

is a portrait of an animal that is awkwardly grooming its fur. The evidence to support this view is a small clump of disturbed hairs in the open mouth of the animal. This remarkable detail, showing a bison straining to nibble at an irritating spot on its flank, is an extraordinarily accurate observation of bison behaviour. It is also significant that this bison, lovingly carved on a small piece of bone, was not intended to be a memorial like those in the caves.

Thousands of miles to the east, at Zaraysk in the Osetr Valley, Russia, a painstakingly crafted sculpture of an adult female bison, carved from a piece of mammoth tusk, has been dated to at least 21,000 years ago. Clearly, the importance of the European bison was not confined to Western Europe alone.

Finally, the world of Palaeolithic bison art has one unique image that deserves a special mention. Found carved into the wall of a limestone rock shelter at Laussel in the Dordogne, close to the famous cave at Lascaux, it shows a plump woman drinking from a bison's horn. Thought to be over 20,000 years old, this relief carving is the best proof we have that the slain bison were used for more than their meat alone. Like the Native Americans

Image of a bison grooming itself, etched on a piece of reindeer antler found at Abri de la Madeleine, Dordogne, France.

we will meet in a later chapter, the Stone Age cave artists were clearly not going to waste any part of their victims' bodies, and there can be little doubt that the animals' pelts were also used for warm clothing, so essential in the freezing world these resourceful, hardy people occupied.

ROCK ART

After the great flowering of art in the Old Stone Age, many centuries pass before the bison appears again as the subject of prehistoric artists. Then, about a thousand years ago, on the rock faces of North America, the American Bison makes its first appearance. The early rock art of the local Indian tribes has revealed that, even far north of its natural range, the buffalo was sufficiently important to be included in the imagery of the red ochre paintings and petroglyphs that adorn the rock surfaces lining the local river systems.

In such regions as Northern Ontario and Manitoba, in Canada, investigators travelling thousands of miles by canoe were able to

The Laussel woman drinking from a bison horn.

detect and record many of these images.[5] Those that were done in rock overhangs had managed to survive the ravages of time and are still clearly visible today. One example was found on a rock wall alongside the Bloodvein River in Manitoba, in the Lake Winnipeg watershed. Although simple in execution, the 'Bloodvein Bison', as it is called, was well proportioned and was obviously drawn by someone who had seen the animal for themselves when they had been living or travelling at least a hundred miles to the south. This portrayal of the bison so far outside its natural range indicates the great significance that the animal must have had for the artist. Although as a work of art the 'Bloodvein Bison' looks rather childish compared with the graceful lines of the European cave artists, the rock artist nevertheless manages to capture the characteristic shape of the bison body, with its heavy chest, its large hump, its head held low, and its horns tightly curled. A special feature of this painting is the presence of a large, clearly defined heart in the centre of the chest. This is a visual symbol of a kind not seen in the cave art of Europe and obviously had some special significance to the artist, although it is hard to guess what this might have been. Was it, perhaps, a kind of target, a symbol saying 'this is where you must strike the animal' when hunting it?

Another interesting detail concerns the shape of the feet. Selwyn Dewdney, the Canadian artist who recorded these rock paintings, makes the following comment:

> A peculiar feature of the feet is the way in which the hooves are rendered as ovals. I was startled to find a few months later, leafing through a book on the Lascaux cave paintings, exactly the same treatment.[6]

As already mentioned, the 'dangling feet' of the hoofed animals in the European cave paintings were shown by Leason to be an

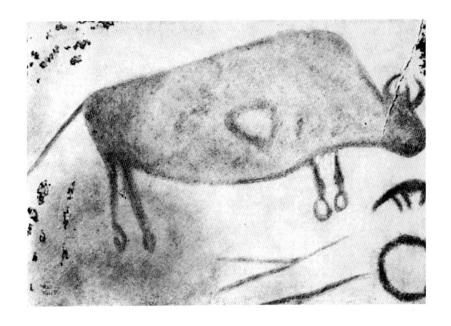

accurate portrayal of feet that were not load-bearing. In other words, they were the feet of slain animals lying on the ground. It is fascinating that the prehistoric rock art of Canada should emphasize exactly the same detail. Even though this particular image must have been made from memory, the artist – no doubt an expert hunter – was able to recall this visual detail with the same sort of accuracy as his earlier, European counterpart. So the 'Bloodvein Bison', like those at Lascaux and Altamira, was also a dead specimen, the victim of a triumphant hunt.

A second bison, this one at Whitefish Bay in Ontario, was less accurate and the feet were omitted altogether, but the great bulk of the animal when seen from the side was captured perfectly. And again, the head is shown in its correct, lowered position, with two small, curved horns and an ear above it.

Hunted Anasazi bison, Newspaper Rock, San Juan County, Utah.

One of the earliest images of bison being hunted from horseback is carved into the rock surface of a sandstone cliff at a site known as Newspaper Rock in Indian Creek Canyon, San Juan County, Utah. Probably dating from the seventeenth century, it was made by an artist of the Ute tribe. The rider appears to be holding a bow that has been fired and a small white line protruding from the front of the bison's hump suggests an arrow has already found its mark. The site is called Newspaper Rock because the 650 petroglyphs created there over a period of 2,000 years read like a newspaper of past events in tribal history. The arrival of horses in the New World with the Spanish conquistadores must have provided an enormous boost to the bison-hunting activities of the local native tribes, an improvement that was duly recorded on the rocks.

Searching the dense panels of petroglyphic images at Newspaper Rock, it is possible to find another bison image placed close to other animals, humans and magical figures. Despite its sketchy simplicity, its large hump and lowered head with curled horns clearly identify it as a bison.

More bison appear at various rock art sites in Utah but they are never particularly common and do not appear in herds, as one might expect. Instead each bison seems to be treated as a particular individual. In one instance, at McKee Springs in Utah, two bison do appear close together, but they are treated differently and do not appear to be connected in any way, merely juxtaposed. The upper bison has a rounded hump and belly, while the one below has an angular hump and a more rectangular body shape. Also, the treatment of the heads differs, suggesting that they were incised by different artists. Only the legs show a similar style.

One of the most controversial images of a bison was discovered recently at the rock art site of Sand Island on the San Juan River,

Schematic bison among the many images at Newspaper Rock, Utah.

near Bluff, Utah. Rock art investigator Professor Ekkehart Malotki and archaeologist Henry Wallace have identified a schematic petroglyph there as representing a bull bison mating with a mammoth.[7] The identification is based upon details such as the bifurcated trunk tip of the mammoth, which they suggest a forger would not know about, the height (5 m/16 ft) of the petroglyphs above the present-day ground level, and their weathered condition. They say: 'The bison may represent a late-Pleistocene *Bison antiquus*.' As regards the mammoth, they comment that

> Several diagnostic features unequivocally point to the portrayal of a *Mammuthus columbi* or Columbian mammoth. Facing left, the animal's dome-shaped head is marked by a solidly pecked top-knot, which rules out identification as a mastodon. . . . The tusks, neatly aligned in parallel fashion, are relatively short and may be a sign that the artist intended to portray a young or female animal. The overlong trunk, shown in profile, may indicate that the artist was overly impressed by it.

The petroglyph is large – nearly 90 cm (3 ft) long – and is so strangely schematic that, on its design alone, it is highly unlikely to have been the work of a modern faker. There is little doubt that it is genuine, but there are some puzzling features. It is not clear why the mammoth's body should be made up of five more or less equal segments, or why the highly characteristic elephant-ine legs have been omitted. The great hump of the bison's body, its lowered head and small, curved horns are all convincing enough, but the mammoth does require a leap of faith, despite its typically domed head, forward-pointing tusks and its ridicu-lously long trunk. If this really is a bison, symbolically coupling with a mammoth, then it must have been created at least 10,000 years ago, before early man in the New World had exterminated all the mammoths that he found there.

There is evidence that mammoths and Palaeo-Indians were living side by side in the region where this strange petroglyph was made, and various dating methods of nearby fossils have suggested that it was 'most likely cut in the rock sometime between 13,000 and 11,000 calendar years ago'.[8] If this is indeed the case, then this must mean that the Sand Island bison is the earliest representation of the animal known in the New World.

2 Bison in European History

Unlike many well-known animals, the bison hardly registers in the ancient civilizations of Egypt, Greece and Rome. The reason is simple enough – its stronghold was too far north. Because of this it was largely spared the indignities heaped on thousands of other large beasts at the Roman games in the Colosseum. But the Romans were amazingly resourceful when seeking exotic animals to display, fight, torture and slaughter, and the great European bison did not escape entirely. There are reports that a few of them were, indeed, rounded up and dragged off to be humiliated for the amusement of the Roman audience. There is even a mosaic that records this fact.

We know very little about how many bison were victims of ancient Roman bloodlust, but the Roman poet Martial mentions that the famous *venator* Carpophorus was brave enough to confront one in the Colosseum, and several other authors, including Pliny, Senaca and Dio Cassius, all reported seeing the 'shaggy-backed bison' in the arena. Pliny remarks that the source for these animals was the Germanic region to the north.

One report of the brutal displays put on in the Roman arena does give us some idea of how the bison were treated. It seems that they were, in fact, the original victims of the lethal combat that still plays out today in Spain and elsewhere – the bullfight. This form of entertainment was first introduced by the Roman emperor Claudius, largely because it was cheaper than many other displays. Aurochs, the now-extinct ancestors of our domestic cattle, and European bison were captured and then released into the arena. Around the central space of the ring were wooden barricades of the kind still used in Spanish bullfights. *Bestiari* 'dodgers' would hide behind these and then rush out to taunt the animals. When they successfully provoked a reaction, they would slip behind a barricade and leave the angry beast to charge at it with its horns. On one occasion a barricade was struck so violently by an enraged animal that a long splinter of wood was smashed from it, whereupon it sailed through the air like a spear and killed a member of the audience. Significantly, it was always the bison, rather than the aurochs,

A bison being dragged to the Roman games in a 4th-century AD mosaic in the Villa Romana del Casale at Piazza Armerina, Sicily.

that caused the most panic, because they were able to gallop much faster and the dodgers had to run for their lives.

Repeatedly provoked, the animals soon became so agitated that they started attacking one another. On one occasion a bison whirled on an aurochs bull and managed to toss it up into the air. When the aurochs crashed to the ground the bison attacked again, skewering it through the eye with its horn. The horn snapped off inside the skull of the aurochs, which died where it lay on the sand. The bison trotted off, victorious. A Roman lady witnessing this dramatic event became so excited that she tore off the priceless brooch she was wearing and, in a moment of wild abandon, threw it into the arena. Alarmed at this extravagant gesture, her male companion leapt into the ring to retrieve the brooch, but the bison spotted him and, spinning round, charged at him, killing him instantly.[1]

At the time of the Roman Games, roughly 2,000 years ago, the loss of the few bison taken for use in the Colosseum would have made no difference to the thriving wild population. In the wild, they were breeding safely right across the great belt of temperate forest that stretched from Britain in the west to Siberia in the east. It would be several hundred years before excessive hunting by meat-hungry Europeans would start to reduce their numbers. By the eighth century this decline was already serious, but worse was to come.

In the twelfth century, land clearance for farming began on a large scale and this continued for several hundred years so that, by the beginning of the sixteenth century, the European bison had disappeared from Britain, Sweden, Italy, Spain and Portugal. The process continued, gaining pace over the next 400 years until, by the twentieth century, the wild European bison that had roamed the land in vast numbers in ancient times was no more.

During the earlier centuries of European history, the bison made surprisingly little impact as a subject for art or craft. It was the bull that became the subject of myth, legend and art, rather than its more exotic cousin. The bison may have been feared, hunted and respected but it was not immortalized. An exception to this was a magnificent ship created by the Norwegian King Olaf that he named the *Visund* – his word for bison. It is recorded that Olaf had this ship made in the winter, and that it was larger than any other. On its prow was the gilded head of a bison and on its stern-post was a bison's tufted tail. In AD 1035 this ship was inherited by Olaf's son Magnus, who assembled a fleet of 70 vessels and set sail to conquer Denmark. As a Norse saga records: 'Olaf has raised a bison's head, / Which proudly seems the waves to tread. / While o'er its golden forehead dashing / The waves its glittering horns are washing . . .' and '. . . southward now the bright keel glides; O'er the white waves the Bison glides.' Furthermore, 'The white foam lashing o'er the deck, / Oft made the gilded head to shake' and 'I can relate how through the gale, / The gallant Bison carried sail. / With her lee gunwale in the wave, / The king on board, Magnus the brave!'[2]

With the other Viking vessels probably displaying more modest figureheads of dragons, the king's bison-headed vessel must have appeared especially menacing. It was huge, needing 30 banks of rowers, and must have looked magnificent with its figurehead, its tail and both sides of the ship gilded over. It certainly seemed to have the desired effect because, when Magnus arrived in Denmark, instead of having to do battle, he was immediately welcomed as their new ruler.

Between the eighth and the eleventh centuries, the Vikings repeatedly sailed out to 'trade, raid and invade' the coastal regions

The popular image of the Viking marauder, re-encountered in a German street festival, 2011.

around their Scandinavian stronghold and beyond. They became infamous as sea pirates, notorious for their rape-and-pillage approach to all they met. At some point their legend acquired the tradition that they appeared as snarling, bearded giants wearing fearsome helmets adorned with a pair of bison horns. Today, nobody attending a fancy dress party as a Viking would turn up without a bison-horned helmet. What is more, when the Vikings were getting worked up to make one of their raids, it was 'well known' that they drank greedily from a bison horn: 'Old Rane the helmsman, whose fierce mustaches and shaggy shoulder-mantle made him look like some grim old northern wolf, held high in air the great bison-horn filled with foaming mead.'[3]

A statuesque Viking with horned helmet in Gimli, Manitoba, a town with a population of predominantly Scandinavian ancestry.

According to modern scholars, the plain truth is that the Vikings never went into battle wearing bison horns on their

helmets. It is claimed that if the marauders wore helmets they were either made of thick leather, or were of simple conical shape that offered better protection for their heads. To have allowed any sort of sharp protrusion from their helmets in close combat, it is argued, would have put them at a serious disadvantage, giving their opponents something to aim at or with which to dislodge their protective headgear.

If this is the case then where did this entrenched and endlessly repeated idea of bison-horned helmets come from? The answer seems to be that we owe it largely to Richard Wagner's costume designers. In one of his operas, *The Ring of Nibelung*, the character of Brünnhilde is a shield-maiden, a servant of Odin. As such,

Ragnar the Viking, the official mascot of the Minnesota Vikings football team, based in Minneapolis.

Arthur Rackham's Hagen with horned helmet, from his re-telling of Wagner's stories in *Siegfried and the Twilight of the Gods* (1911).

she wears a suit of armour and a bison-horned helmet, and it is this helmet that seems to have caught on as a visual image, and been repeated ever since, whenever a Viking is conjured up in modern times. As one historian put it: 'Within just a few decades the headwear had become synonymous with Vikings, enough to become shorthand for them in advertising.'[4] Part of the confusion may have stemmed from an archaeological discovery made in 1942 at the Danish town of Vekso near Copenhagen. During peat digging in a nearby swamp a pair of bronze helmets with large, protruding horns was discovered, dating from the 900 to 1100 BC. These much earlier horns appear to have been worn purely for ceremonial purposes, rather than in battle, but their existence may have fuelled speculation about the form of the later Viking helmets and been used to support the bison-horn theory.

There, matters might have rested, with the much-loved bison-horn Viking helmet consigned to oblivion as a fantasy of fictional origin. But there is a sting in the end of this story because new evidence has been unearthed in northern Scotland proving that some Vikings, at least, did indeed wear horned helmets into battle, although not in the form that the popular imagination has envisaged them. Grave goods in a Viking Age boat burial at Hinty Gock on the island of Hrossey included a badly damaged helmet with two open sockets on either side of its conical dome, each still containing fragments of horn. The shock detail revealed by this helmet is that the horns were not worn side by side, as in a living bison, but instead where placed one in front of the other on the Viking's head. The front horn was worn downwards in such a way that it provided a powerful nose-guard. The rear horn was worn upwards, supposedly as a signal to other Vikings to identify a man as one of theirs in a confused situation. So, in the end, it seems that the bison horn did, after all, play a part in this brutal period of human history.

THE BESTIARY BISON

Moving on to the Middle Ages, the European bison now puts in an appearance in a highly stylized form and with a singularly unpleasant way of defending itself against its enemies. In the early bestiaries that were compiled in the twelfth and thirteenth centuries, the bison is given the name of Bonnacon or Bonasus. Even though it has a mane and inward-curling horns, it is only just recognizable as a true bison, although that is what its name tells us it must be (see page 11). It was said to be extremely dangerous because, when pursued or attacked, it reacted by shooting burning dung at its enemies. This action appears in all the bestiaries wherever this animal is illustrated.

The bestiary compilers all appear to have taken this tale from the much earlier writings of the Roman author Pliny the Elder who, in his great *Natural History* of AD 79, describes a huge bison-like creature with a shaggy mane. He emphasizes that the animal's horns bend inwards to such a degree that they cannot be used for fighting. This mistaken idea leads him on to suggest that the Bonasus, or Bisonte, as he calls it, must have other means of defending itself. He mentions two, the first of which is 'good footmanship'. The second defence mechanism is the one that seems to have appealed so strongly to the bestiary writers. In Philemon Holland's 1635 translation of Pliny it is referred to as 'dunging', when the bison 'will squirt out from behind him three acres in length' faeces that are so hot that they 'burneth them that pursue him, like fire'.[5] The dunging distance of 'three acres' has been interpreted elsewhere as 7.3 m (24 ft) – a prodigious effort even for a bison in full flight. One of

Horned helmets (like these from a Danish hoard) were probably worn for ceremonial purpose.

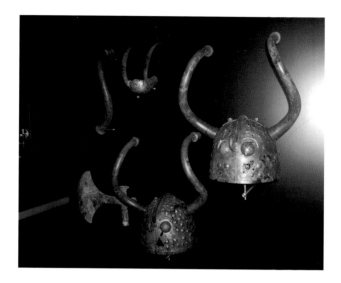

the twelfth-century bestiaries goes even further, saying of the dung that 'any tree that it reaches catches fire'.[6]

It is amazing that this bizarre tale of a bison defending itself by squirting burning dung should have survived for so long and that Pliny's authority on such matters continued to influence authors more than a thousand years later.

BISON IN THE EARLY NATURAL HISTORIES

Following this period, the appearance of more serious natural histories in the sixteenth and seventeenth centuries revealed that the bison was still unfamiliar, anatomically speaking. The Gómara bison of 1554 was a charmingly deformed creature with an exaggeratedly shaggy coat and exceptionally large hooves.[7] All that can be said for its depiction after three centuries is that it had, at least, stopped shooting burning dung at its enemies.

Francisco López de Gómara's bison of 1554, with huge dewlap, shaggy coat and enormous feet.

The *bonnacon*, a mythical relation of the bison, from an English bestiary of *c.* 1200.

atqɜ ꝑetiuuſ qui uꞇ nũquã reũdatur. naturalꞇ
capſulaꞃum modo clauditur: ꝺ ʙoʜaꞇoʜ.

ʜ aſia
am
malnaſ
cit̃ qꝺ
bonna
con di
cunꞇ.cu
tauꞃm̃
caͫp. ac
deinceꝑ
corpuſ
omne
camꞇum

Topsel's bison of 1607, with an improved body-shape.

The mid-17th-century bison of Aldrovandi, still in a primitive form.

opposite: Jonston's three types of bison illustrated in 1657.

Tab. XVII

Bisons Magnus

Bison Iubatus

Locobardus
Bison

Perhaps this was because the Gómara bison was meant to be the American species, about which different tales and traditions prevailed. Gómara was a Spanish priest who never visited the Americas but who wrote about them at length, basing his descriptions on information he had obtained from those who had made the great journey to the West. His having never seen an American bison accounts for its odd appearance. It was, however, the very first picture of the American animal to be published in Europe.

Matters had improved slightly by the beginning of the seventeenth century, when Edward Topsel offered a more naturalistic animal in his *History of Four-footed Beasts*.[8] However, although the shape of the body was improving, the horns were still hopelessly inaccurate. Worse still, in his text Topsel reverts to some of the earlier tales and legends, including the myth of the dung attacks, even elaborating it by offering a scientific explanation for this strange behaviour. He explains how the contents of the bison's entrails, being heated by the chase, become dangerously hot. Also, because the fleeing animal's alimentary canal becomes restricted, it starts to suffer from 'wind in the gut'. This combination leads, eventually, he says, to a 'violent eruption' so powerful that the dung 'may fly far backward' and, if it strikes a pursuing dog, or a man for that matter, it scorches the hair and burns the skin. Instead of rejecting the story, Topsel embroidered it.

Strangely, in 1642 Aldrovandi, in his great thirteen-volume natural history, fails to improve the body shape and even returns to a more primitive form of bison, probably copied from Gomara's earlier version.[9] A little later, in 1657, Jonston makes a step forward by offering three different kinds of bison, although it is not at all clear which types these are meant to represent.[10] He calls them The Great Bison, or *Bison Magnus*,

The Maned Bison, or *Bison Jubatus*, and The Slow-moving or Slow-witted Bison, or *Locobardus Bison.*

In the eighteenth and nineteenth centuries, with the rapid advance of scientific natural history, the bison at last became more accurately portrayed and the animal shown in the *British Cyclopaedia* of 1835 is more clearly recognizable.[11]

THE HUNTING OF THE EUROPEAN BISON

While these gradual improvements in the bison literature were taking place, the animals in the wild were suffering more and more from increasingly well-armed hunters and from the loss of their natural habitat. The urbanization of Europe, the destruction of the great forests, the rapid increase in human population and the spread of settled farming, with fences, walls and hedges slicing up the countryside, all meant that the European bison's days were numbered.

In ancient times there had been bison all over the Continent, from the British Isles in the west to Siberia in the east, and from Scandinavia in the north to the Iberian peninsula in the south. The western regions were the first to lose their bison. This had happened by the eighth century. In northern Scandinavia they had gone by the eleventh century and in southern England by the twelfth. In Hungary they became extinct by the sixteenth century and in Romania and most of Russia they lasted until the eighteenth. In some regions they were protected as royal game

The aftermath of a bison hunt in Hungary.

and several attempts were made to keep them in enclosures, breed them and then turn them loose for hunting. But even these efforts had limited success because of the activities of poachers. An irony often encountered with large game animals like the bison is that it was only the rich hunters who really helped them. If they wanted to enjoy the heady sport of big game hunting they had to have enough animals to kill. The bison's worst enemy became his closest friend. If the bison vanished, so did the thrill of the chase.

One of the last strongholds of the European bison was the great, primeval forest of Białowieża in Poland. This magnificent woodland was one of the remnants of the ancient forest that used to cover the whole of Europe before human development changed the face of the Continent. For centuries, the wild herds living in it were the property of the Polish kings and in the six-teenth century the monarch imposed the death penalty on any-one killing a bison without permission. Following political changes involving the partition of Poland in 1795, the Russian tsars took over the protection of the bison in the nineteenth century. In order to keep the forest as a thriving hunting reserve for the Russian nobility, Tzar Alexander I employed expert herd managers supported by 150 guards. When this new phase in bison history began there were fewer than 500 of them in the entire forest, but by the middle of the nineteenth century this figure had risen to nearly 2,000. All seemed well, but then upheavals in the region, combined with a plague of leaf-eating caterpillars, saw the numbers plummet until, by the end of the century, the herds had shrunk again. It is recorded that by 1889 there were no more than 380 left.

When the twentieth century dawned a survey revealed that, in the whole of Europe, wild bison now survived only in the Białowieża forest and in parts of Russia's northern Caucasus.

Even there, the numbers were pathetically small. These precious survivors now faced a new threat with the outbreak of war in 1914. The Białowieża forest was occupied by German soldiers who had no inhibitions about slaughtering the wildlife they found there. A count of bison in the forest in 1915 revealed that the herd there had risen to 785, but 600 of these were soon killed by the soldiers for meat or merely for sport.

By the end of the war, in 1918, there were only nine bison left alive. In the aftermath of the war, even these were taken and by the end of 1919 the bison was extinct in Poland. Now, only a few remained in the wild, in the Caucasus. When these, too, were killed by poachers in 1927 the European bison finally became extinct as a wild animal. At this point we would have lost this magnificent animal for ever, were it not for the fact that a few were still living in zoos. Anticipating the end of the wild survivors, in 1923 zoo authorities set up the Society for the Protection of European Bison. A quick count of the captive bison revealed that there were only 54 animals to act as the foundation stock for a carefully controlled breeding programme.

All was going well when, once again, war broke out and threatened their survival. This time, however, steps were taken protect the animals. In 1939 there were only 30 living in the Białowieża forest, in breeding stations, and another 34 in captivity in Germany. The death penalty was once again introduced for the killing of a Polish bison and three German soldiers were executed for shooting one. When the war ended in 1945 the species was still in existence, but only just. In Poland there were now only 24 and in Germany, thanks to Allied bombing, only twelve. The European bison was once again hanging by a thread.

Help was at hand with a massive shift of attitude towards wildlife, thanks to the growth of the conservation movement in the second half of the twentieth century. By the end of that

Modern bison hunting.

century there were over 3,000 European bison in existence. Following the success of the carefully planned breeding programme in zoos, it was at last possible to release some European bison into the wild again. Białowieża forest could once again boast a herd of 800 animals and this time they were reasonably safe because the region had been designated a UNESCO World Heritage Site, a UNESCO Biosphere Reserve and an EU Natura 2000 Special Area of Conservation. A 2004 report records a world total of 1,800 free-ranging and 1,400 captive European bison alive at that time.

In 2012 it was announced that a German aristocrat was taking the imaginative step of introducing a herd of eight bison to live wild in his 32,124-acre (13,000-ha) forest in Westphalia.

They had been kept in an enclosure in the forest for some time and were finally released in April 2013. If they survive and start breeding successfully, they will be the first wild bison herd in Western Europe for 400 years.

With a more enlightened approach towards wildlife in the twenty-first century, there is the real chance that the wisent may once again become a common species, although it has to be noted, with regret, that big game hunters are already at work again, posing for trophy photographs over the carcasses of the bison they have just slaughtered. With their high-powered rifles and little need for risk-taking, these modern trophy hunters can hardly be described as sportsmen. In spirit, their killings are cotton-wool adventures. One of them, from Denmark, was shameless enough to remark, 'I took my bull from a luxury high seat blind that had windows and heat, which was nice, considering it was cold.' One of the hunting companies tempts its clients by offering accommodation 'in a beautiful house in the middle of the forest' where 'traditional dishes of the Polish cuisine are served' and there are hunting ceremonials 'like playing hunting horn signals' and festive meals around the campfire.

These hunting companies publish price lists that reveal that it costs thousands of euros to kill a bison. You are punished if you fail to make a clean kill, because there is an item that reads 'Wounded and lost bison: 4200'. Clearly these are not skilled marksmen of the old school, but modern urban gun-lovers.

It might seem inconceivable that this has happened so soon after the painstaking resurrection of the species, but the free-ranging population has increased from 1,800 to 2,700 during the ten years between 2004 and 2014, and there are now about 2,000 in captivity, worldwide. This has emboldened authorities in such places as Belarus and Poland to allow limited culling by wealthy hunters. If this culling was being done because the populations were growing too fast for the regions where they are now allowed to roam free, or to weed out sick or injured individual animals, it might be acceptable to modern conservationists, but if the culling is being done for the fun of downing a powerful beast, it will be seen simply as the fostering of a long-rejected attitude to wildlife that most members of the public today would oppose.

At the last count, apart from animals scattered around the world in zoos and animal parks, the main concentrations of European bison today are as follows.

Belarus:	958
Caucasus:	500
Poland:	1,300
Russia:	461
Ukraine:	240

3 Bison in American History

Our relationship with the European bison goes back a long way. There is evidence that our ancient ancestors, using long spears, were hunting large prey in Europe 400,000 years ago and bison was no doubt a favourite item on prehistoric menus. We have direct visual evidence of this from about 25,000 years ago on the cave walls of France and Spain. Our relationship with the American bison is much more recent, because the earliest human intrusion into the vast, virgin territories of North America did not occur until about 13,000 years ago. Then, when the sea levels were low and a land bridge had opened up in the Bering Strait between what is now Siberia and Alaska, some of the northern Asian tribes ventured across and made the first, tentative explorations of what would prove to be an exciting New World.

Pushing south, these earliest Americans will have encountered huge herds of a bison species that had previously faced little competition. The ancestral species, the steppe bison, had made the journey across a much earlier land bridge and had had plenty of time to adapt to this new environment. Once in North America it had evolved into several new species, one of which, *Bison antiquus*, may have met up with the very first humans to arrive, but it was replaced on the Great Plains about 9,000 years ago by another species called *Bison occidentalis*, the Western Bison. This we know for certain was hunted by human tribes, until it too was replaced, this time by the modern American bison, *Bison bison*. This new species, differing only slightly in appearance from the European bison, was immensely successful, multiplying into a thriving population in the extensive woodlands and across the grasslands of North America. In Europe and Asia the bison had faced competition from other species of wild cattle, but here it was the only one – bison alone having made the dangerous crossing from Siberia.

THE BISON AND THE AMERICAN INDIAN

For the advancing tribes of these first Americans – the Palaeo-Indians – these bison herds must have been a welcome sight. Those pioneering human groups that settled in the woodlands and on the plains of North America would soon come to rely on this species as their key to survival. Its herds not only supplied their food, but also skins for clothing and for dwellings. But humans were thin on the ground at this stage and the bison were plentiful, so a balance was achieved. The new predators were able to kill as many bison as they liked without causing any serious damage to the herds.

Once a tribal kill had been made, the bison carcass was carved up for many uses. Records suggest that there were as many as 65 different ways in which the American Indian tribes would utilize a dead bison. These can be summarized as follows:

FOOD The flesh of the bison provided a high-quality meat that was the main source of protein. In addition, humans also ate the tongue, the testicles, the bone marrow, the intestines and other internal organs. They dried some of the meat to consume as pemmican in the winter months. They drank the blood and any milk they found. Special delicacies were raw brains, raw liver and raw nose-gristle. Skin-scrapings were mixed with berries to make a jelly. Pounded bones were boiled, the grease skimmed from the surface and put into bladders, from which it was used as a kind of butter.

CLOTHING Hides were cut and stitched to make costumes for both adults and children. They were also used to fashion caps, moccasins and mittens. Snowshoes were made from sinews. Hide with hair was employed to make gloves and ceremonial robes. Headgear made of horns and hair was worn on special occasions.

WEAPONS Arrows and arrow-straighteners were made from ribs, and arrow-points from horns – to be used against the

Charles Vogel, engraving after Karl Bodmer, 'Herds of Bisons and Elks', illustration for Maximilian, Prince of Wied, *Travels in the Interior of North America, 1832–1834* (1839–41).

Bison horns, hair and hides worn on ceremonial occasions, here by a Sioux chief c. 1900.

species that supplied them. Bow-strings were made from sinews. Shields were created from tough hides. When horses were introduced as an aid to hunting, the saddle-covers were made from hide and the whips from tails.

UTENSILS Cups were made from hide, hooves and horns. Horns were also employed in the making of spoons and ladles, and also a variety of containers including tobacco holders and medicine holders. Other containers were made from the intestines. Hide was used to make kettles, carrying cases and water bags.

DWELLINGS Tepees were covered in hides, webbing and thread were made from sinews, rope and yarn from hair and bedding from hide with hair attached.

HOUSEHOLD GOODS The rough surface of the bison's tongue was used as a hairbrush, its tail as a fly-swat, its hair to stuff pillows and cushions, its long bones to make tools, its shoulder blades to make hoes, its gallstones as a source of yellow pigment, its fat to make soap, its dried dung as fuel for the camp fires, its penis and its boiled bones to make glue, its brains as a hide-softener during tanning, its fat as a paint base, and its teeth and hair to make ornaments.

CEREMONIES Bison dung was sometimes used for ceremonial smoking sessions, and bison skulls were employed during tribal rituals. For ceremonial music, rattles were crafted from hooves and drums from hides.

Karl Bodmer, *Sioux Tipi*, water-colour to illustrate Maximilian, Prince of Wied, *Travels in the Interior of North America, 1832–1834* (1839–41).

VEHICLES The hide was used for covering canoes and on the Indian travois, which was a kind of sledge dragged along the ground, usually by travois-dogs of a special breed.

So, for the tribal Indians killing a bison was like visiting a supermarket. It would be wrong, however, to imagine that a bison hunt was an everyday event. There was plenty of small game available which was much easier to catch with primitive weapons. For the earliest Americans, a bison hunt would have been a special occasion, a dramatic tribal challenge and, if successful, the cause for a great celebration and feast. Because of

George Catlin, *Bull Dance, Mandan O-kee-pa Ceremony*, 1832, oil on canvas.

this there slowly grew a cultural mythology that endowed the bison with special powers. By embellishing and exaggerating such powers, tribal storytellers were able to make bison-kills even more memorable.

Because the Indian hunters knew how difficult it would be to kill a bison, they prepared themselves for the event by offering prayers, conducting rituals and performing dramatic dances. It was hoped that these actions would bring them good fortune in the forthcoming hunt. If a particular hunt failed this would be blamed on a failure to have performed the rituals correctly, rather than on any errors made by the hunters in the field. In this way, the champion hunters of a tribe could maintain their high social status regardless of results. There were all kinds of secrets and mysteries linked to hunting success and failure. Some of the ceremonial dances were conducted to bring the herds nearer. Sacred stones were kept that were believed to have a magical influence over the herds. Tobacco-smoking rituals were also performed.

As the centuries passed, an elaborate network of indigenous tribes developed with complex mythologies and local customs, deeply reliant on the bison herds for their survival and for their prosperity. The ecological balance between the early American Indians and the plentiful bison lasted for thousands of years, until white settlers arrived from Europe in the sixteenth and seventeenth centuries. Their appearance on the scene would drastically alter the ancient balance and see the bison suffer more and more.

There were three phases to the hunting of bison by indigenous peoples. The first phase, lasting from 13,000 years ago until the arrival of the Europeans, involved hunting on foot. The second phase involved hunting on horseback with spears and arrows. The third phase, after the indigenous tribes had acquired firearms from the Europeans, involved hunting on horseback with rifles.

In the first phase, several strategies were employed. One was ambush, in which the human hunters crept up on the unsuspecting herds, sometimes employing animal skins as camouflage. Another technique was box burning, involving the surrounding of a herd and setting grass fires on all four sides of it. Hemmed in by the flames, the bison could be driven into a smaller and smaller area and, in the chaos that ensued, were easy to kill. A European traveller crossing the plains in 1804 observed whole herds of bison with fur that was charred from these Indian assaults.

Another method was stampeding, in which hunters created panic in the bison herd that sent them headlong over a cliff or onto an icy surface where they were almost helpless. If the herd could be driven onto a frozen lake, they would find it impossible

George Catlin, *Buffalo Hunt under the Wolf-skin Mask*, 1832–3, oil on canvas.

to gallop without slipping and the hunters had them at their mercy. An alternative in winter was to drive them into deep snow where, again, they would struggle to move at speed. Recent excavations near Denver in Colorado have revealed that a tribal hunt which took place there about 8,500 years ago involved stampeding a herd of bison into a gulch and, once they were trapped there, slaughtering them.[1] The experienced Indian hunters would make use of any natural feature of their environment to drive a herd of bison into a location where the formidable galloping speed of the animals could not save them. Stampeding was a dramatically effective way of hunting the bison, but it was also a wasteful one. Frequently, there were far more bison killed than were needed at that moment by the Indian tribe. The hunters would take what they wanted and leave the rest to rot. It seems that they did not worry about this, simply because there were so many bison available to them. There was no pressure on them to be careful hunters.

Alfred Jacob Miller, *Hunting Buffalo*, c. 1859, watercolour.

This type of killing appears to contradict the idea that the Indians made use of every bit of the bison they killed. The explanation would appear to be that both wasteful and efficient hunting styles will have taken place at one time or another, according to the local circumstances. If, for example, a drive resulted in a dozen dead bison, the hunters might take everything they wanted from just a few of these and leave the rest to rot. They would use 'every bit of the bison' but not, perhaps, 'every bit from every bison'.

The arrival of horses, obtained from Europeans, made hunting with spears and arrows much easier and the tribesmen soon

Indian hunters
driving bison over
a precipice.

developed remarkable skills as agile riders that made their bison kills much easier. On horseback they could, at last, keep up with the fleeing herds and, balancing deftly on their steeds, aim their weapons at the weak spots of their victim's anatomy. Whereas hunting bison had been a very special event and a huge challenge, it now became more routine and changed the nature of the Indian cultures that were involved. Some of the Indian tribes acquired horses in the seventeenth century, others as late as the middle of the eighteenth century. In the seventeenth century, Spanish settlers in what is now New Mexico, then homeland of the Pueblo and Navaho Indians, were employing Indians as lowly manual workers on their ranches and these labourers began to learn how to handle, train and care for the imported European horses they found there. The original, American horses that had inhabited the continent thousands of years before had become extinct at about the time the first Palaeo-Indians arrived across the Siberian-Alaskan land bridge. They were wild horses and if the first humans in the New World had encountered a few of them they would have treated them as prey, just like the Palaeolithic cave people had done 20,000 years previously in France. Using them as domestic animals – as steeds and as beasts of burden – was something entirely new to the Indian tribesmen. When they saw the way the Spanish intruders used their horses, they quickly recognized their value and, as slave labourers, learned all they could about this fascinating animal. In the past, when a nomadic tribe moved from one location to another, most of their worldly goods were dragged along on travois sledges, pulled by the tribal dogs. This was a cumbersome business and using horses would clearly make life much easier, if only they could have them for themselves, rather than having to service those of their new Spanish masters. The Spanish must have realized that these

John Mix Stanley,
*Buffalo Hunt on the
Southwestern
Prairies,* 1845,
oil on canvas.

thoughts were passing through the Indians' heads, because they soon introduced a law to make it illegal for an Indian to own a horse.

This was the situation through most of the seventeenth century until, in 1680, the Pueblo Indians had had enough of their servitude and attacked the Spanish, driving them south into Mexico. Many of the horses were left behind in the chaos and now, at last, the Indian tribesmen had their own treasured, equine possessions. It would be fourteen years before the Spanish returned and during that time the Pueblo were able to start breeding horses and trading them with other tribes, such as the Comanche. The excitement at owning and riding these new animals was infectious and horses spread far and wide through more and more tribal groups. They rapidly became a way of life for the American Indian.

Charles Vogel, engraving after Karl Bodmer, 'Indians Hunting the Bison', illustration for Maximilian, Prince of Wied, *Travels in the Interior of North America, 1832–1834* (1839–41).

Charles Russell, *Buffalo Hunt No. 10*, 1895, oil on canvas.

This use of the horse continued to spread over the next 50 years, with some tribes, such as the Cheyenne, not acquiring them until the middle of the eighteenth century. The animals were not always Spanish in origin. In one region, British traders entered the scene and exchanged horses for Indian products such as dried meats and furs. By late in the eighteenth century virtually all the Indian tribes of the west had horses. This new phase in Indian hunting meant that the bison became more and more vulnerable, but worse was to come.

While the horse had been spreading to the north and the east through more and more tribes, another major innovation was spreading from the northern territories down towards the south and the west. This deadly novelty was the introduction of firearms. When the Indian tribes first encountered the guns of the Europeans they viewed them as weapons of 'wonder'. They immediately saw these firearms as a means to hunt bison with much greater ease. And it did not escape them that if they could acquire both horses and guns, then their hunting efficiency would be dramatically increased. The situation was complicated, however, because there were so many separate tribes, some on friendly terms, but others at war with one another. At first, the acquisition of horses and guns was therefore scattered and erratic. Some tribes had horses but no guns, others had guns but no horses and still others had neither.

The situation with the Europeans was also confused. In some regions there were local laws prohibiting the trading of firearms with the Indians. It had occurred to some of the newcomers that the guns might one day be used against them, instead of against the bison. Punishments were severe and included heavy fines, whippings and imprisonment. In other places, trade was commonplace. The Europeans wanted pelts and furs and were happy enough to exchange them for guns, for a special reason. It was clear that the more guns the Indians had, the more bison they could kill and the more pelts would become available for trade. So trading continued and laws were ignored.

Despite the official prohibitions, the eighteenth century saw a widespread revolution in the bison-hunting techniques of the Indian tribes. As the use of horses spread more and more from the south and the use of guns spread down from the north, it was inevitable that eventually these two innovations would meet and then overlap until, right across the grasslands of the American plains, the herds of bison had a lethal new enemy to face – an American Indian hunter on horseback armed with a gun. This situation continued into the early part of the nineteenth century and tribal hunting became so easy that the herds might have suffered, were it not for the fact that the indigenous population was still quite small.

THE GREAT EUROPEAN SLAUGHTER OF THE AMERICAN BISON

At the start of the nineteenth century there were still millions of bison roaming the vast, wild expanses of North America. A dark cloud on their horizon, however, was the increasing number of new European intruders, bringing with them their own domesticated cattle and a tradition of settled farming. Fixed-location farming and wild hunting have always clashed and now there would be a clash of horrific proportions.

It was clear that, with their now refined hunting techniques, the Indian tribes were thriving, using bison both for their own needs and also for increasingly prosperous trade. For the early white traders in furs and pelts, this was a highly satisfactory situation, but for the new farmers and homesteaders it present-ed a threat to their very survival and was a problem that had to be overcome. If they were to take the land from the Indians and secure it for their domestic livestock, two things had to happen. The Indians had to go and the bison had to go. As the success of the Indian tribal cultures was so dependent on the bison, the simplest solution was to destroy the bison herds. Although simple in concept, in practice it was more daunting because of the huge numbers of animals involved. How could you possibly slaughter millions of bison to make way for the new, farmed landscape? The task seemed insurmountable, but nevertheless, this is the gruesome task that was begun in the 1830s.

Although it seems almost inconceivable, in the 60 years that followed, at least 30 million bison were killed by the immigrant European population of North America. Some authorities put the total figure even higher, but whatever the precise number, it was the most brutal slaughter of wildlife in the history of the human species. Nothing else comes close. The perpetrators had no shame. They felt no remorse. At the peak of the massacre, an

The 19th century sport of bison-shooting from passing railway trains; here, the Kansas-Pacific Railroad, in the 1870s.

American general in Washington proudly announced that, once the American bison have been exterminated, the Indians will be controlled and civilization will be able to advance. A congressman from Texas put it slightly more diplomatically by saying that, in his opinion, the civilization of the Indians would benefit if there was not a single bison in existence. He may have chosen his words carefully, but his true motives were clear enough – to destroy existing Indian culture.

In 1870, at the height of the bison slaughter, the great Mark Twain, in 'The Noble Red Man', added his voice to the discrediting of the American Indian: 'He is ignoble, base and treacherous, and hateful in every way . . . His heart is a cesspool of falsehood, of treachery, and of low and devilish instincts.'[2] With their literary heroes writing in such tones, it is not surprising that the immigrant Europeans were happy to see the destruction of the staple food of the Indian – the unfortunate bison. With words of encouragement like these, military commanders were soon ordering their troops to open fire on the bison herds, not for sport or for produce, but simply to deny them to the Indians. One general went on record as saying that this strategy had been more effective in a few years than 'sending in the cavalry' had been over half a century.

In the 1860s great railroads were built from east to west, cutting through the wild territories of the bison herds. This had three devastating effects: it disrupted the natural movements of the herds; it offered a moving platform from which train passengers could take pot shots at bison, often just for the fun of it; and it provided a quick way to ship massive amounts of bison products from the west to the east. Because the bison herds were so large, they often blocked the railway tracks and specialist bison-killers, like the infamous William Cody, known as Buffalo Bill, were brought in to deal with this problem. At the same time, he

Buffalo Bill Cody, who became famous for his mass slaughter of bison, photographed in a New York City studio in the 1880s.

provided meat for the railway workers. He claimed to have shot 4,282 bison in eighteen months. A rival of his, William Comstock, also wanted to be known by the name of Buffalo Bill. To avoid confusion, the two men agreed to take part in a competition to see who would have the sole right to use the title. The contest took the form of an eight-hour shoot-out to see who could kill

A mountain of bison skulls at the Michigan Carbon Works, Detroit, photographed with evident pride, mid-1870s. The bones would be made into bone-ash fertilizer or printing ink.

A mountain of buffalo hides at Rath & Wright's hide yard in Dodge City, Kansas, in 1874.

the most bison in that time. Cody shot 68 with his favourite rifle, which he called Lucrezia Borgia, while Comstock only managed 48.

Some of the most gruesome images in the long history of man's callous cruelty to animals emerge from the nineteenth-century bison massacre. A photograph, proudly taken of a huge heap of skins, or, worse still, a proud pose by bison-workers by a mountain of bison skulls, gives some idea of the scale of the destruction.

To give a few examples:

- An estimated 2 million bison were killed in 1870 on the southern plains alone.
- A railway engineer claimed that, in 1873, you could walk a hundred miles by stepping from one bison carcass to another.
- At auctions in Fort Worth, Texas, 200,000 bison hides were being sold every few days in 1874.

A hide-hunters' encampment in Texas, in the mid-1870s.

- In 1872, 1873 and 1874 an average of 5,000 bison were killed every day. Ten thousand hunters were at work on the plains.
- In 1871, one firm alone in St Louis traded no fewer than 250,000 bison skins.
- No fewer than 1.5 million bison hides were packed onto freight trains in a single season – the winter of 1872–3 – to be shipped east.
- When hunters made mass kills, the local homesteaders would collect the bones left behind and sell them at about $8 per ton for making fertilizer. In Kansas alone this brought in 2.5 million dollars between 1868 and 1881. This represented the remains of at least 31 million bison.
- In 1881 one county alone in Montana shipped out 180,000 buffalo skins, during the slaughter of the northern herd.

By the end of the nineteenth century, the vast herds of American bison had vanished. Between 30 and 60 million of them had been massacred in a period of little more than 60 years. In 1902 it was estimated that there were only 700 left, all in private herds, and a last remaining wild group of 23, now carefully protected in the Yellowstone National Park.

From this small remnant the species would now have to survive under human control. The American Indian tribes suffered a similar fate. Their ancestral lands were now almost entirely taken over by white homesteaders, with the result that the remnants of the native populations, like the bison, were being kept in protected reserves. The struggle was over; the European immigrants had won.

RECOVERY IN THE TWENTIETH CENTURY

Like the European bison, the American bison was facing extinction early in the twentieth century, but as with its Old

World relative, it was brought back from the brink by a few concerned individuals. In 1905 the naturalist Ernest Baynes founded the American Bison Society to protect the surviving animals. William Hornaday, the director of Bronx Zoo in New York, was its first president and Theodore Roosevelt was its honorary president. At the time, Theodore Roosevelt was president of the United States, and Baynes was not shy about approaching him for support. He clearly impressed Roosevelt who, in August 1905, wrote to Baynes saying, 'I congratulate the buffalo upon having such an efficacious man as you to champion him.'

One of the first actions of the Bison Society was to set up a National Buffalo Herd in Oklahoma. The animals were collected from zoos and private parks, Bronx Zoo sending fifteen from its collection. The small herd was established in the 60,000-acre (24,000-ha) Wichita Mountains Wildlife Preserve and this has been recorded as the first ever wild animal reintroduction to have been undertaken in the United States. The herd is still there today and now numbers about 650.

In 1935, with bison in America and Canada now numbering in the thousands, the American Bison Society felt that its work was done and that the American bison was, at last, safe for the future. So they held a meeting at which they voted the Society out of existence. However, in 2005 it was relaunched because it was clear that there were still problems to be solved in relation to preserving the ecosystem of the bison. The new Society's official aim is given as restoring 'the bison's ecological role as an important species in the North American landscape over the next century by working with government agencies, conservation groups, ranchers, Native American groups, and others'. In addition to this it is 'calling on the federal government to better coordinate management of bison across federal lands, and work with Canada and Mexico on cross-border bison management'.

The problem today is not so much the numbers, but their management. There are now over half a million American bison in herds across the United States and Canada, but 500,000 of these exist as part of commercial projects based largely on meat production, and often involving interbreeding with domestic cattle. These commercial bison are housed today on 4,000 privately owned ranches. It has been estimated that no more than 30,000 bison are kept in non-commercial herds where the main objects are conservation and scientific study. Of these, only about 15,000 are truly wild and not fenced in. A meticulous survey carried out at the start of the twenty-first century revealed that, although there are as many as 65 of these non-commercial herds, the majority of them are very small, ranging from ten up to a few hundred.[3] Those with 300 or more animals, consisting of genetically pure-bred bison living under more or less natural conditions, are limited to 26 locations. They are as follows:

Major Herds of Plains Bison in the USA
1 The Antelope Island plains bison herd in the Antelope Island State Park at Great Salt Lake, Utah (700 animals)
2 Badlands National Park plains bison herd, South Dakota (750 animals)
3 Clymer Meadow Preserve plains bison herd, in the Blackland Prairie region, near Greenville, northern Texas (300 animals)
4 The Custer State Park plains bison herd in the Black Hills of South Dakota (1500 animals)
5 Delta River plains bison herd, Alaska (400 animals)
6 Farewell Lake plains bison herd, Alaska (400 animals)

Rosa Bonheur (1822–1899), *Buffalo en profil*, undated, oil on canvas.

7 Fort Niobrara National Wildlife Refuge plains bison herd, along the Niobrara River in north-central Nebraska (350 animals)

8 Fort Robinson State Park plains bison herd, near Crawford in western Nebraska (500 animals)

9 Grand Teton National Park plains bison herd, north of Jackson, in northwestern Wyoming and south of Yellowstone National Park (700 animals)

10 The Henry Mountains plains bison herd in south-central Utah, north of Lake Powell (400 animals)

11 Medano-Zapata Ranch plains bison herd in the northeastern San Luis Valley, Colorado (2,500 animals)

12 The National Bison Range plains bison herd at the National Bison Range Wildlife Refuge, in Flathead Valley, Montana (400 animals)

13 Niobrara Valley Preserve plains bison herd in Brown and Keya Paha counties of Nebraska (500 animals)

14 Tallgrass Prairie National Preserve plains bison herd in Oklahoma (2,500 animals)
15 The Wichita Mountains Wildlife Refuge plains bison herd, near Lawton in southwestern Oklahoma (650 animals)
16 The Wind Cave plains bison herd in Wind Cave National Park, South Dakota (450 animals)
17 The Yellowstone National Park plains bison herd located primarily in Wyoming, but also extending into Montana and Idaho (3,700 animals)

Major Herds of Plains Bison in Canada
18 The Elk Island plains bison herd in Alberta (500 animals)
19 Pink Mountain plains bison herd in British Columbia (1,000 animals)

Bison living wild today in the Wichita Mountains Wildlife Refuge.

20 The Prince Albert National Park plains bison herd in Saskatchewan, the only free-ranging population of plains bison in a Canadian national park (310 animals)

Major Herds of Wood Bison in Canada
21 Aishihik wood bison herd, Yukon Territory (500 animals)
22 The Elk Island wood bison herd in Alberta (315 animals)
23 MacKenzie wood bison herd, near Fort Providence, Northwest Territories (3,000 animals)
24 Slave River wood bison herd in the Northwest Territories (600 animals)
25 Syncrude wood bison herd near Fort McMurray, northern Alberta (322 animals)
26 Wood Buffalo National Park wood bison herd, in northern Alberta and Northwest Territories (5,600 animals)

All these figures will vary considerably from year to year. The bison herds, protected from predators and monitored for disease, will grow rapidly as each adult female produces her annual calf. In those herds where the available territory is limited – something that applies to most of them – these natural increases will require careful management to avoid over-crowding. This takes three forms. First is culling, second is selling or giving animals to other locations, and third is passing animals over to Indian reservations. This last activity is now organized by the InterTribal Bison Cooperative, as the reservation-dwelling remnants of the once great indigenous tribes regain some of their ancestral food sources.

The important task for the future is to ensure that pure-bred bison are surviving and thriving in conditions as close to their original habitat as possible. Without wild herds in natural environments there will always be a risk that the character of the species will change and its original qualities will be lost.

As so many of the commercially farmed herds now have some percentage of domestic cattle in their genetic make-up, the careful isolation of the conservation herds and the protection of them from contamination is essential. Fortunately, the awareness of this problem is acute and both the plains bison and the wood bison are now in good hands, with numbers on the rise, and appear to be safe for the future.

One extreme proposal, made in 1987, called the Buffalo Commons Project, put forward the revolutionary idea that a vast territory covering 139,000 square miles (88,960,000 acres) of the Great Plains region should be converted back to a wild prairie habitat for bison.[4] This would involve no fewer than ten American states (Montana, Wyoming, Colorado, Oklahoma, New Mexico, Texas, North Dakota, South Dakota, Nebraska and Kansas) and would see the gradual conversion of farms and ranches back into wild prairie grasslands. In the proposal it was argued that the drier parts of the Great Plains region has for some time been in recession with many ghost towns now replacing what had once been busy communities. However, there was considerable resistance to this idea on the part of those landowners who were still active. It remains to be seen whether the gradual exodus from the drier regions of the Great Plains continues and, if it does, whether the thunder of the hooves of vast herds of wild-living bison will once again be heard on the open prairies. Some would see this as a backward step, a case of turning the clock back to the days before the west was conquered and tamed by the early homesteaders. For many others, however, it would be more a case of repaying a huge debt owed to the American bison following its mass slaughter in the nineteenth century. And it has been pointed out that, as a tourist attraction, the sight of herds of hundreds of thousands of bison moving majestically across the grasslands would be a wildlife spectacle with no equal in the twenty-first century.

Today, with the bison safe from extinction and with the protected herds growing larger every year, the urge to slaughter them has once again proved irresistible. American big game hunters have returned to the scene. The justification for this resurgence of sport hunting is that 'public herds require culling to maintain a target population.' It has been pointed out that target populations could also be maintained by selling the animals to zoo parks all over the world, or to private owners with game ranches where the bison would provide an attractively exotic display. But the primeval human desire to gun down large animals seems to be overpowering and reasserts itself as soon as circumstances provide an excuse.

Criticisms of these new hunters have varied from the mildly disdainful to the downright violent. An official of the Humane Society of the United States said that bison hunting today 'affords trophy hunters the opportunity to shoot what are effectively parked cars', adding, 'These bison have no fear of people and will stand and stare in curiosity as they are gunned down.' A spokesman for the Buffalo field Campaign made the same point, saying that the animals 'are too docile for hunting . . . They have little fear of humans, so there isn't much sport involved . . . For them to claim it's a fair chase hunt is a bunch of smoke and mirrors.'

Bison-hunting is also taking place in Canada, despite the fact that voices have been raised in protest there too. Several ranches are offering package hunts with a guaranteed kill. One such ranch, with over a thousand bison in its fenced enclosures, charges U.S.$3,000 for a three-day hunt, with the promise of a dead bull at the end of it. For a further $1,500, a local taxidermist will stuff the bull's head for the hunter to hang on his wall to remind him of his love of nature. Wildlife experts note with satisfaction that, thanks to a shift in public opinion, the demand for bison kills is decreasing rapidly and will probably soon disappear altogether. Hunters claim that, without their financial support, the maintenance of the large herds may suffer. Whatever the outcome of this ongoing debate, it is safe to say that the American bison, like its European counterpart, will never again face complete extinction.

4 Bison as Food

On the commercial bison ranges today large numbers of animals are being killed for their meat and other products. The herds are managed and the animals bred specifically for this purpose. These bison have effectively become domestic livestock and, in contrast to the conservation herds, there is no attempt to keep them pure-bred. Many of them have been crossed with various kinds of domestic cattle to improve meat production. With nearly half a million of these domestic bison alive today, this has become big business.

Bison meat, or buffalo meat as it is often called, is valued for its nutritional quality. Those who market it stress that it comes from animals that have been living on grass and have not been subjected to any drugs, chemicals or hormones. It is illegal to use growth hormones on bison. The meat is said to have a superior balance of protein, fat, mineral and fatty acids, and it has a greater concentration of both iron and essential fatty acids than beef.

Choice beef has more than four times as much fat as bison meat. It also has less protein, more cholesterol, less vitamin B-12 and more calories. The one drawback with bison meat is that, because of the way in which the animals are raised, it is more expensive than the beef from domestic cattle.

These are some of the forms of bison meat that are now being offered for sale in the United States:

The increasingly popular bison burger.

Ground bison (1 lb/450 g package)
⅓-lb (150 g) ground bison patties (1 lb/450 g package)
¼-pound (113 g) ground bison patties (1 lb/450 g package)
Bison brats – regular or jalapeño (1 lb/450 g package)
Bison stew meat (1 lb/450 g package)
Bison roasts
Arm, chuck, rump, round or sirloin tip (2–3 lb/900 g–
    1.35 kg average)
Swiss steaks
Sirloin steaks
New York strip steaks
Rib-eye steaks
Tenderloin steaks (filet mignon)
Bison jerky

Originally bison meat was sold by natural food stores as a health gimmick, but its growing popularity has meant that it is now also available from butchers and mainstream American supermarkets, and bison burgers have become popular in many American restaurants.

All this means that the herds of half a million commercially farmed American bison will continue to grow, at the expense of the more intensely farmed domestic cattle. This will do little to help the herds of about 20,000 conservation-managed bison, but it does reinstate the species as a major food source of the North American continent, a role that it played for thousands of years up until the great slaughter of the nineteenth century.

5 Bison as Emblems

Because of its image as a huge, powerful, stubborn, courageous animal, the bison has frequently been employed as an emblem, symbol, mascot or logo. It appears in heraldry, in insignia, as the badge of many sports teams and as the name of countless commercial products.

HERALDRY

The bison is not commonly used in heraldry. The lion, the eagle, the dragon and the unicorn are far more popular on crests and coats of arms. But the bison is far from absent. For obvious reasons the European bison has a much longer heraldic history than the American bison. On crests and coats of arms it usually goes by its alternative name of wisent. To give two examples: the town of Schleiz on the Wisenta River in East Central Germany acquired a city seal in 1297 that showed two wisent, one in profile on the shield and one rearing up on its hind legs as the crest above the helmet. This design was officially accepted as the city's coat of arms in 1915. Local emergency money produced in the 1920s also showed a version of this 'two-wisent' coat of arms. This local currency, or *Notgeld*, was a response to the rapidly accelerating inflation that led to hyperinflation in Germany in the 1920s, following the end of the First World War. Further to the east, in

City seal of Schleiz on the Wisenta River.

The coat of arms (later version) of the town of Drohczyn.

Manitoba coat of arms, *Gloriosus et Liber.*

Poland near its border with Belarus, the town of Drohczyn was awarded a coat of arms in 1498. In early days this simply showed the head of a wisent on a plain shield, but in the mid-1960s it was changed and made more elaborate. A side view of the whole animal, a bull wisent, was now shown in silhouette. This was retained in several later versions of the town's coat of arms. Below the wisent there is the Eagle of Poland and the Knight of Lithuania, the town having belonged to both these countries in the past.

The American bison is a much more recent feature of heraldic design, but is popular in certain regions of Canada. It figures repeatedly in the heraldic designs of the Canadian province of Manitoba. The coats of arms of the province, granted by Royal Warrant of King Edward VII in 1905, shows one standing boldly on a cliff top, ably aided in the complicated design by a unicorn, a horse and a beaver. On the crest of the lieutenant governor of Manitoba, however, the bison stands defiantly alone.

Heraldic coats of arms are still being designed today and the one created for the Rural Municipality of Macdonald, Sandford, Manitoba in Canada was introduced as recently as 2007. It shows two bison guardant, supporting the shield, standing on a grassy mound and displaying bright blue horns. The motto *Perseverate et florete* means 'persevere and flourish', an appropriate comment in relation to the North American bison.

INSIGNIA

Outside the realm of heraldry, the bison also appears as a central feature of the official insignia of a number of organizations. One of the most famous of these is the Royal Canadian Mounted Police. A bison's head has been present on the badges of the

90

Mounties for more than a century, first appearing in 1876. The details of the design have changed several times since then, but the bison has always retained its central position. The choice of a bison as the focus of these insignia is appropriate because of the strong historical link between the Mounties and the grasslands of the Western prairies. Today, with police cars replacing the traditional horses, the latest insignia can be seen emblazoned on the doors.

The badge of the 12th Manitoba Dragoons.

Other bison insignia in Canada include the flag of Manitoba, granted royal approval by Elizabeth II in 1965, the University of Manitoba in Winnipeg and the badge of the 12th Manitoba Dragoons. It also appears on the badge of the police in the town of Altona, Manitoba, although it is easy to miss it there because for some reason it is shown in dark brown on a black background. Although much smaller, it is more visible on the badge of the police in Manitoba's second largest city, Brandon. It seems as if, when you travel around the Canadian province of Manitoba, you will be confronted with emblems of bison wherever you look.

Heraldic badge of the Royal Canadian Mounted Police, introduced in 1954.

Canada is not alone in flying a bison flag. In the United States, Kansas and Wyoming have adopted the bison as their official state mammal and it appears on their state flags. The Wyoming State flag, adopted in 1917, shows a bison branded by the great Seal of Wyoming. The Kansas State flag, adopted in 1927, shows a landscape that includes a herd of bison fleeing from two Indian hunters on horseback. The bison is also the state mammal of Oklahoma but does not appear on their flag.

The state flag of Wyoming displaying American bison.

These are just a few of the hundreds of bison insignia that appear in many parts of the world. The characteristic silhouette of the animal that makes it immediately recognizable, even in a very simplified form, and the obvious symbolism of its power

and strength make it the ideal emblem for a wide range of organizations.

SPORTS CLUBS

Because the males charge headlong at one another it was inevitable that many sports teams would adopt the bison as their badge. There are literally hundreds of bison teams around the world. A small sample is as follows:

Basingstoke Bison	Ice hockey club in England
The Bisons	NCAA teams of Lipscomb University, Nashville
The Bisons	NAIA teams of Oklahoma Baptist University, Shawnee
Bisons de Neuilly-sur-Marne	Ice hockey team in Neuilly-sur-Marne, France

Bristol Bisons RFC	English rugby union team
Bucknell Bison	Athletic teams of Bucknell University
Kentucky Bisons	American Basketball Association team
Manitoba Bisons	Athletic teams of the University of Manitoba, Canada
North Dakota State Bison	Athletic teams of North Dakota State University
Okotoks Bisons	Ice hockey team in Okotoks, Alberta, Canada
Wainwright Bisons	Ice hockey team in Wainwright, Alberta
FC Zimbru (= Bison)	European football club in Chisinau, Moldova
Buffalo Bandits	National lacrosse league, Buffalo, New York
Buffalo Bills	American NFL football team, Buffalo, New York
Buffalo Bisons	Minor league baseball team, Buffalo, New York
Buffalo Gladiators	Semi-pro American Football team, Buffalo, New York
Buffalo Sabres	Ice hockey team, Buffalo, New York

COMMERCIAL PRODUCTS

The use of the bison as an emblem of a commercial company or product is widespread. As the bison is physically so powerful, it tends to represent the power of a company or the strength of its product. The great bison massacre is forgotten and the symbolism focuses instead on its commanding muscular presence. It is not surprising therefore to find the bison employed as the logo of hard liquor, such as Bison Vodka and

Bison as the emblem of Żubrówka vodka.

Bison Canadian Whisky. Bison Brewing in Berkeley, California uses a logo that shows a bull bison staring at a basil plant while a bee buzzes around its head, to advertise its Honey Basil Beer. A Californian fruit association also enlists the head of a bison, presumably to send a subliminal message about the strength of the flavour of its products. In the realm of clothing, Bison Country Wear has the same sort of message – their products are tough enough to stand the wear and tear of country living.

Companies using the name bison are too many to name. There are literally hundreds of them, covering everything from Bison Planks to Bison Stairlifts, Bison Engineering, Bison Designs, Bison Manufacturing and Bison Rooftops.

For some it is not enough simply to use the bison as an emblem of their product – the product itself has to be made of bison. With so many of the animals now being killed commercially for their meat, it means that there is once again a large amount of bison hide available and this is being used in furniture, clothing and even as the covering for exotic vehicles.

The owner of a modern ranch house in Texas decided to give it an unmistakably American atmosphere and achieved this with the help of large quantities of American bison hide. All the furniture was finished in bison leather while the stuffed head of a bison gazed down at the scene from above the fireplace. The bison upholstery incorporated special boot-stitching that was inspired by the patterns seen on cowboy boots. In the bedrooms, the beds were given bison leather headboards and the floors were covered in 'laced bison robe carpets'.

In the realm of transport the name Bison has often been used. Perhaps the strangest example is the Second World War German armoured vehicle known as the Sturmpanzer I Bison. Employed during the invasion of Poland, it was essentially a tank chassis mounted with a huge gun. Because this gave it a massive, 'big-chested' shape, it reminded the Germans of the silhouette of the

Bison-themed furniture in an Arizona furniture showroom.

big-chested bison and that became its nickname. More recently, the Canadian Army operated an armoured personnel carrier produced in 1989 by General Motors in Ontario that was given the name of Bison. Quite a number of vehicles have been given the name of bison in an attempt to emphasize their power and strength. There are too many to name them all, but a few examples are: the Bravado Bison, a large, double-cab pickup truck; the 2011 BMW 5-Series F10 'Black Bison' By Wald International; the Bison Chevrolet heavy-duty truck; and the Bison Savanna pickup truck, manufactured by the Beiqi Foton Motor Company in China.

In 2013 a group of Russian designers calling themselves The Workshop of Functional Luxury, decided to convert a hatchback Peugeot into a unique display of bisonry. They covered the entire body of the vehicle with hand-stitched bison skin, stripped from the carcasses of nearly a dozen Canadian wood bison. This hide was processed so that it would stand the scorching heat of Middle Eastern summers and the freezing cold of the winters of Russia.

They covered all the interior surfaces of this unique bison car, from dashboard to boot, in cured leather. Bizarrely, the engine is also lined with bison leather that was specially treated for added heat resistance. The seats are finished in treated leather and lined with bison fur to keep passengers warm on long winter drives. Even the petrol nozzle and the interior of the boot have been coated in hide. As a final touch, they employed master engravers from the Middle East to carve a series of inscriptions on the hide. They are now trying to sell the car through a Russian auto-trader for the sum of 40 million roubles (£784,000).

Another strange, bison-themed vehicle is a customized motorcycle designed to make it appear that the rider is sitting not on a bike but on one of the animals. This conversion was carried out at the Black Hills Harley-Davidson centre in Rapid City, South Dakota and was displayed at their annual motorcycle road show in 2012.

6 Bison as a Visual Image

The European bison has been more popular than the American bison as a subject for postage stamps. There are two reasons for this. First there are more European countries that feel an association with bison, even if that association is rather slender. In North America there are only two countries involved. Also, in North America there may be a lingering sense of embarrassment about the way the bison was treated in that region in the past. The bison may be an American icon, but it is also a stark reminder of the greatest animal slaughter in the history of mankind.

COINS

In North America, the image of the bison has been engraved onto coins in both the United States and Canada. In Europe it has appeared on coins minted by Poland. Different engravers have treated the image in different ways. Some have preferred the close-up of the head, while others have favoured the whole body of the animal seen in profile, or two bulls headbutting, or a herd stampeding.

In the United States there are two notable bison coins, the ordinary five-cent coin, first minted in 1913, and the special-issue gold coin with a face value of $50 that did not appear until 2006. The five-cent coin, known as a nickel, was designed by the American sculptor James Earle Fraser to showcase the history of the American West. On the other side of the coin there is an engraving of the head of a Native American chief. The $50 gold coin is the only pure, 24-carat gold coin ever struck by the u.s. mint. It was intended as a convenient way to own pure gold in the form of legal tender that was guaranteed by the u.s. Government.

In Canada there are also low- and high-denomination bison coins, the first produced by the Canadian Mint as recently as 2011, the second, even more recently, in 2013. The low-denomination coin shows a modernist design of the bison with a coloured patch behind it representing the moon. Canada is the only country to produce general-circulation coins with coloured details of this kind. The high-denomination coin, designed by Claudio D'Angelo and valued at $100 (Canadian dollars), shows a herd of bison stampeding across the prairie. The other side of the coin features a portrait of Elizabeth ii designed by Susanna Blunt.

In 2003 the National Bank of Ukraine issued silver coins depicting the European bison. Designed by Volodymyr Demyanenko, one was worth two Ukrainian hryvni, the other ten hryvnas. In 2012 the National Bank of the Republic of Belarus issued a pair of special silver coins dedicated to the European bison, each with the value of twenty roubles. One of them features the image of two European bison with Swarovski crystals inlaid as their eyes. The lettering indicates the animal's name in Belarusian and Latin. The other side of the coin bears the coat of arms of Belarus. The second coin shows only the head of a single bison, also with inlaid crystals forming the eyes. They also minted a more valuable gold version of the latter, with

The 30 cents u.s. bison postage stamp, 1923.

The 5,000-ruble bison postage stamp, Belarus, 2008.

The u.s. bison nickel, 2005.

Canadian silver $100 bison coin, 2013.

Polish *wisent*
(bison) coin,
20 zloty
denomination.

a value of 50 roubles. Finally, Poland has issued two bison coins, one worth two zloty and the other twenty zloty. They were both minted in 2013. So many of these bison coins have very recent issue dates, suggesting that the bison is coming into its own now that conservation efforts are succeeding and the revived herds are at last on the increase.

ART

The bison has fared badly in the world of high art. Whereas the domestic bull has featured time and again in the work of great artists, notably Pablo Picasso, the bison has somehow seemed too exotic to become a favourite subject. Its image is so strong, its silhouette so characteristic, that it has failed to appeal to those artists who might wish to mould it to their own style.

Ukrainian 10
hryvni bison coin
issued in 2003.

Belarus silver
20-rouble bison
coin minted in
2012.

Pen-and-ink
drawing of a
European bison
by Albrecht
Dürer, 1501.

A badger, a lion and a bison in the Garden of Eden, in a woodcut by
Albrecht Dürer, 1509.

The only great master to have portrayed the bison is the German Renaissance artist Albrecht Dürer (1471–1528), and even he managed only a half-finished sketch.[1] He met the bison when five of them were presented to King Maximilian during a visit to Nuremberg in 1501. Dürer was obviously fascinated by these rare beasts and noted in his diary that 'they looked very strange'. From his drawing, now in the British Museum in London, it is clear that he was intrigued by the fact that their coats were much longer and shaggier at the front of the body than at the rear. A few years later, in 1509, Dürer rather quaintly included a bison in his woodcut of *The Fall of Man*. While Eve is busy persuading Adam to take the apple that the serpent is offering, the bison kneels at her feet with its head cocked to one side. In his engraving of the same subject made five years earlier the kneeling figure is not that of a bison but of a domestic bull, lacking the long

Hand-coloured lithograph after George Catlin, *Buffalo Bull Grazing*, c. 1845.

shaggy hair. Why he should have changed his mind and given this role to the bison is not clear. According to a Dürer expert, this 'European bison symbolizes melancholic gloom'.[2]

The only time since the cave art of the Palaeolithic that the bison has been a popular subject for artists is the nineteenth century, when a number of American artists, attempting to capture the drama of the Wild West of the United States, repeatedly portrayed the American bison facing up to its deadly human predators. These melodramatic, academically executed paintings form a genre that falls short of high art, but that nevertheless has carved an important niche as part of the ethnographic history

George Catlin, *Wounded Buffalo, Strewing his Blood over the Prairies*, 1832–3, oil on canvas.

of America. The most important figures in this school of art are George Catlin, Alfred Miller, John Stanley, Albert Bierstadt, Charles Russell and Edgar Paxson.

American self-taught artist George Catlin (1796–1872) became obsessed with American Indian culture. He opened an Indian Gallery to show his work and even toured with it across North America and Europe. He tried to persuade the American government to acquire his collection as a record of the society of the first Americans, but failed. The early nineteenth century was a time for the suppression of Indian culture, not its celebration. Fortunately his works were saved for posterity and are now highly regarded, although they are more valued as historical illustrations than as works of art.

John Mix Stanley,
The Buffalo Hunt,
1845.

John Mix Stanley (1814–1872) was the most unfortunate of the American painters of the Old West. In 1842, inspired by the work of George Catlin, he travelled to the southwest to study and paint the Indian tribes there. He showed great promise and was exhibited at the Smithsonian, but sadly more than 200 of his paintings and all his maps and records of his trips were destroyed in the disastrous Smithsonian fire of 1865. He never fully recovered from this and was largely forgotten until recent times when his few surviving works were re-evaluated.

Albert Bierstadt (1830–1902) was a German-American artist of great technical ability and probably the most accomplished of all the nineteenth-century artists who set about depicting the American West. At his peak he was immensely popular and his canvases sold for huge sums. He was famous for his dramatic use of light and shade, although some felt that it was excessive. He was also criticized for his theatrical style and his work eventually fell out of favour, although more recently it has been re-evaluated.

Charles M. Russell (1864–1926) was a cowboy and wrangler for many years, absorbing first-hand as much as he could of 'The Old West' before settling down to become an artist, recording all he had witnessed during his early years. His paintings enjoyed considerable popularity, largely because of their narrative style, each one capturing a particular moment in the dramatic lives of inhabitants of the 'Wild West'. 'Kid' Russell, as he was known, lived long enough to see his work collected by the first great movie stars of Hollywood westerns such as Will Rogers and Douglas Fairbanks.

A friend of Russell's was the artist Edgar Paxson (1852–1919) who had a similar passion for the Old West. On his death, Russell summed him up by saying: 'His work tells me that he loved the Old West . . . and today the west that he knew is history that lives

Charles Marion Russell, *Buffalo Hunt (no. 40)*, 1919, oil on canvas.

in books. His brush told stories that people like to read . . . The iron heel of civilization has stamped out nations of men, but it has never been able to stamp out pictures, and Paxson was one of the men gifted to make them.'[3]

While the European Americans were recording their version of the Wild West in the nineteenth century, the native Indian tribespeople were also creating their own artwork. Bison skulls and hides were employed as surfaces on which to paint their images and bison sometimes also figured as subjects in the paintings themselves, usually when a bison hunt was being depicted. Early examples of these art forms have been known to fetch six-figure sums at auction in the United States in recent years.

The painting of bison hides has a long history with Native American tribes and is an art form that is still being executed today. The images are sometimes abstract and geometric, like the 'feathered sun' design, sometimes descriptive, showing members of the tribe in their various costumes, and sometimes narrative, showing bison hunts, tribal battles or ceremonial dances. Some of the designs, given supernatural values, were said to be inspired by visions and dreams. One of the best-known tribal hide painters was Cadzi Cody (1866–1912) of the Eastern Shoshone tribe. He was active in the latter part of the nineteenth century and his favourite scene consisted of a sacred Sun Dance, shown in the centre of the hide, surrounded by a bison hunt. He was the first Indian artist to sell his painted hides, after he was confined to the Wind River Reservation. When he discovered that visiting European Americans, who had come to witness the Sun Dance, would pay good money for them he began to modify the details to make them more appealing. This was the very first move towards commercializing the ancient tribal designs.

In addition to bison hides, bison skulls were also employed as a suitable surface for painting sacred signs. These decorated skulls

Edgar Samuel Paxson, *Buffalo Hunt,* 1919, oil on canvas.

A painted bison robe, Mandan tribe, *c.* 1830.

were used for religious ceremonies and were thought of as the channel by which prayers could be transmitted to *Wakan Tanka*, the Great Spirit. Some were also placed outside the dwellings to act as a protection against evil forces. The most extraordinary example of a painted bison skull was discovered by archaeologists in 1994. Dr Lee Bement was digging in a location where between 30 and 50 bison had been killed with spears after a herd had been driven into a narrow gulch by Palaeo-Indians of the Folsam culture. As he gently brushed the earth away from one particular skull he saw to his astonishment that a zigzag line had been painted on it

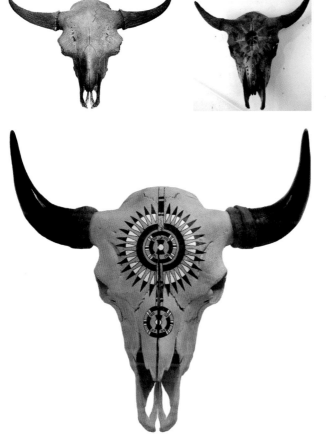

The oldest known work of art in the Americas: a painted bison skull.

Bison skull decorated by a member of the Sioux tribe in the 19th century.

Modern tribal example of decorated bison skull.

in red ochre. What made this discovery so extraordinary was not the image itself but its date. For the Folsam culture had flourished between 9000 and 8000 BC and this simple red zigzag is the oldest known example of human art in the whole of the Americas. It shows that native rituals involving decorated bison skulls have the

Tribal slaughter of a herd of bison: *Lakota Bison Jump* by Peggy Detmers.

longest history of any American art form. Ten thousand years later, the Sioux and other American-Indian tribes were still decorating these skulls and a few examples still survive, including one with a red, black and yellow sunburst pattern.

The tradition of painted bison skulls is still being carried on in the twenty-first century, although today it has a more commercial air attached to it, for these skulls are not displayed on native camp sites but on the walls of elegant art galleries where they fetch high prices. The symbols may still have ceremonial roots, but the driving force behind their production is now more fiscal than spiritual.

One of the most impressive modern representations of the American bison is the bronze assembly piece called *Lakota Bison Jump*. It measures 46 x 30 m (150 x 100 ft), took over six years to create and has been installed at an outdoor museum just outside Deadwood. The work of American artist Peggy Detmers from South Dakota, it is more than life-size and shows a herd of bison being driven over a clifftop to their deaths by a band of tribal American Indians. It is a monumental piece comprising no fewer than seventeen huge figures – fourteen bison and three mounted Indian hunters – and dramatically captures the moment when this grotesquely wasteful method of bison-hunting reaches its lethal climax. It was commissioned by Hollywood actor Kevin Costner. For Native Americans this sculpture has a special significance, not because of the way it recreates one of their early hunting strategies, but because it also brings to life one of the great tribal legends, the story of how the sacred Buffalo Dance began. The tale begins with a time of hardship, when the bison were refusing to be driven over the cliff tops and the tribe was going hungry. The proud daughter of one of the hunters went to the bottom of the cliff and sang a song to the bison, offering herself as the bride of the strongest bull if the herd would leap over the cliff to feed her tribe. The herd plunge to their deaths except for the strongest bull, who lands on top of the others and is unhurt. He picks the girl up in his horns and takes her away to be his bride. Her father comes to rescue her but the herd trample him to death. His daughter sings another of her magical songs over one of his

Franz Marc, *Red Bison (Bison in Winter)*, 1912, oil on canvas.

bones and it brings him back to life again. The herd is amazed and offers to teach her tribe the Buffalo Dance which, if they perform it before a hunt, will ensure their success. In exchange she has to promise to sing her song over their bones that will bring them back to life again.

A modern artist who has depicted bison is the German Expressionist Franz Marc. His *Red Bison* shows animals with exaggerated colouurs. A contemporary Canadian artist, Marion Rose, goes further. In her paintings the anatomy of the bison is realistic, but they are dramatically multi-coloured. Instead of the typical dark and light brown of the living animal, Rose's bison are dark and light blue with the addition of red and orange. Colorado artist Tracy Miller, who calls her style Contemporary

Western Expressionism, goes further, with even wilder patches of colour, but still retains the natural outline of the animal. This idea of keeping the bison's iconic shape, but dramatically modifying its colouring, seems to be the solution for a number of modern artists when faced with the challenge of portraying this animal. With many other animals, such as dogs, cats, birds or fish, it is possible to manipulate the basic shape, to exaggerate, suppress, abstract or play with it in various imaginative ways, and yet still keep the origin of the image detectable in each case. This is not so with the bison. Its silhouette is so specific, so immediately familiar and so unusual that to tinker with it renders it unrecognizable. However, if the characteristic outline is kept, then it is possible to play wantonly with its colour scheme. Even with the most outlandish colour patterns it will remain recognizable as a bison.

This was made very clear when, early in the twenty-first century, a craze developed in North America for painting life-size fibreglass figures of bison in very bright colours and displaying them in public places. This craze began in the year 2000 when the city of Buffalo saw 153 of these colourful bison figures scattered around its public places. Called the *Herd About Buffalo* art project, it was done to raise money for a local medical centre. It was initiated by Patricia Wilkins, who saw a similar exhibit in Chicago and said, 'I immediately envisioned life-size fiberglass buffalos roaming our great city.' Local artists were enlisted to decorate the 2.1-m (7-ft) long, 1.5-m (5-ft) tall fibreglass animals and to locate them around Buffalo. They were later auctioned off, with the proceeds going to the Roswell Park Cancer Institute. Sadly, Patricia Wilkins herself died of cancer before seeing her project completed.

The idea caught on and brightly coloured bison started to appear in other places in the United States. To give two examples,

in 2005 in Custer, South Dakota, a local public art project,
involving twenty life-sized fibreglass bison, was called *The Custer
Stampede*. Each animal was painted by a different artist and they
were placed at various public locations such as Rapid City Airport,
Custer State Park and Mount Rushmore National Memorial. The
following year, in Fargo, North Dakota, a similar project, with 50
painted bison, was called *The Herd About the Prairie*, and was
described as a Virtual Art Stampede. In the city of Buffalo itself
the project was repeated in 2010, albeit on a smaller scale, again
to raise money for a good cause.

In complete contrast, Belarusian artist Roman Beybutyan
from Grodno takes all the colour out of his bison images. His
life-size metal bison is made entirely from spare car parts.
Unlike Marion Rose, who spent a great deal of her life in the

114

Bison statue, Gallaudet University, Washington, DC, 2010.

The world's largest buffalo monument near Jamestown, North Dakota.

field studying bison in their natural habitat, Armenian-born Beybutyan has never seen a living bison. He worked entirely from a photograph of one, welding the car parts together until they resembled the animal as closely as possible. He used shock absorbers, springs, steering rods, clutches, chains and various parts from Soviet-era cars collected from neighbours' garages and from local scrapyards. The sculpture took three months to assemble and the artist's wish is that it should eventually stand in the Białowieża Forest, where European bison are once again living in the wild, under the watchful eye of conservationists.

Beybutyan may not have realized it, but he is part of a modern art movement called Metal Yard Art that is made up of artists who create sculpture from scrap metal. Bizarrely, the bison is one of their favourite subjects. In France, Pierre Matter creates what he calls Steampunk Sculpture from copper, bronze, brass and steel. He was born in Munster in the Alsace region of France, where he became obsessed with machines. As raw material he uses recycled and scrap materials including cogs, pistons, integrated circuits and other fragments of the industrial world. Near Augusta, Georgia, in the United States, Franklin Jensen also uses scrap materials to make his life-sized sculptures. He began working with scrap iron in 1978, but his bison was unusual in that it was created from strips of redwood decking. Another American artist, Lou Willie, fashioned his life-sized bison almost entirely from polished chrome car bumpers. Made in 1989 and called *Chrome on the Range II*, it has been exhibited on a concrete platform in downtown Grand Junction, Colorado. American sculptor John Lopez grew up on a ranch in South Dakota. He already had a successful career working in bronze when he began to experiment with scrap-iron sculpting. He found a way to merge the two art forms and called it Hybrid Metal Art, blending iron and bronze. Lopez was able to build a career as an artist without ever having to abandon his isolated prairie home in South Dakota.

In the world of comics, cartoons and computer games, the bison is nearly always depicted as the epitome of savage violence and brute strength. The commercial artists who create these images seem to equate the forequarters of the bison with the upper body of a professional wrestler. It is almost as though, unconsciously, they are allowing this massacred and maltreated animal to take its revenge. In the gentler world of cartoons, the bison is rarely depicted, but just occasionally one can be found acting as a shy or cuddly creature with a friendlier disposition.

7 Bison as Companions

Taking care of bison in captivity has not been a popular pursuit. Bison have never been favourites in zoos and have rarely been tamed as working animals, pets or performers. From time to time, however, there have been exceptions to this rule and there are some interesting historical records of these activities.

BISON IN ZOOS

Most of the European bison taken to ancient Rome were destined not to be cared for in captivity as beasts of wonder, but to be slaughtered in the arena for the entertainment of the baying urban crowd. There were, however, a few proper zoos kept by powerful figures where the animals were looked after as a spectacle to be enjoyed. In the third century, for example, Gordian III had a spectacular menagerie that contained 32 elephants, 60 lions, ten tigers and ten giraffes, not to mention hippos and rhinos and many other species.[1] Some of these early zoos will no doubt have included European bison.

In the Middle Ages we know that European bison were kept in early menageries and we even have a description, written in 1523, of how they were caught in the wild to be shipped to their new homes: 'Two walls were placed widely apart, but narrowing down as they lead forward into a kind of tight wedge.'[2]

At almost exactly the same time, Europeans first set eyes on the American bison. This event took place in the zoo belonging to the Aztec ruler, Montezuma II. The year was 1521 and the Spanish explorer Cortez had just reached the Aztec capital of Tenochtitlán. There he discovered that the monarch had maintained a well-run zoo for the pleasure of his people. Staffed by 300 keepers, it contained many exotic beasts, but the most prized of all was something called a 'Mexican Bull'. It is clear from the description of this animal that it was in fact an American bison:

> In the second Square . . . were the Wild Beasts . . . among which the greatest Rarity was the Mexican Bull; a wonderful composition of divers Animals. It has crooked Shoulders, with a Bunch on its Back like a Camel; its flanks dry, its Tail large, and its Neck cover'd with Hair like a Lion. It is cloven footed, its Head armed like that of a Bull, which it resembles in fierceness, with no less strength and Agility.[3]

It is not surprising that this animal was considered such a great rarity, because the nearest bison habitat was over 400 miles to the north of the Aztec capital and the Aztecs lacked any sort of wheeled transport. How they managed to catch the animal and deliver it to Montezuma's zoo over this distance is something of a mystery. The fact remains, however, that this was the very first time that Europeans had met a live American bison face to face.

In the centuries that followed, zoos all over the world became more and more commonplace until almost every major city had one. Bison were featured in many of them but never had the crowd appeal of such favourites as lions, tigers, elephants and giraffes. The reason seems to have been that they were all too often exhibited singly or in very small groups in cramped quarters. The drama of the bison herd was absent and visitors passed them by.

London Zoo received their first American bison in 1829. It was a young female presented to the zoo by the Hudson's Bay Company, the world's major fur-trading business. They acquired their first European bison a little later, in 1847, when the Tsar of Russia gave them a pair. One of these lived for a year, the other for eighteen months. As these are remarkably hardy animals, this does not say much for the conditions provided for large ungulates at the zoo in those early days. Their capture in the Białowieża Forest and transportation to London was an epic undertaking. Tsar Nicholas I, having been told of 'Queen Victoria's wish to have two living bisons in the London Gardens' instructed his master of the Imperial Forests, Dimitri Dalmatoff, to see to it that this was done. Dalmatoff decided that the best solution was to acquire two very young bison calves and then rear them with domestic foster-cows. 'At dawn on 29th July, 1846, he set forth on his task, accompanied by three hundred beaters and eighty foresters, the latter armed with guns charged only with powder, so as to alarm but not damage the bison.'[4]

Dalmatoff later wrote a whole paper on what happened next, as if it were some sort of medieval battle. He recorded in detail the way in which the herd did their best to protect the calves, with the bulls putting themselves between the hunters and the young ones. But with the blowing of the hunter's horn, the baying of the hunters' dogs and the advance of the beaters, sufficient confusion was created so that it was possible to secure four calves, a male and three females. Of these, the male, who was described as 'morose', and one of the females, were dispatched to London and Dalmatoff became the proud recipient of London Zoo's first ever silver medal.

Since the dramas of those early zoo days, animal husbandry has advanced dramatically and today bison are housed successfully in many zoos, usually in large enclosures where they can live in more natural social groups. When London Zoo opened Europe's first park-zoo at Whipsnade in 1931, a herd of American bison were among the very first exhibits. Their huge hillside enclosure, clearly visible from nearby roads and known locally as 'bison hill', became a much loved landmark and when, in the 1990s, the bison herd was removed from it, the zoo received so many complaints that they had to put the animals back.

BISON AS DRAUGHT ANIMALS

As early photographs show, American bison have occasionally been harnessed as draught animals, pulling small carts, but this mode of transport was never more than an exotic novelty, and

Pair of bison pulling a cart, illustrating a U.S. postcard of 1910.

bison generally managed to avoid this particular form of exploitation.

BISON AS STEEDS

Bison do not take too kindly to being saddled and ridden, but a few brave souls have attempted this feat and lived to tell the tale. Some of them, like Dick Bishop from Hugoton, Kansas, who rode a bison called Grunter as part of the Kansas State Centennial in 1961, reduced the risk of injury by mounting an animal that had been de-horned. Cowboy Vern Elliot of Platteville, Colorado, was less cautious, galloping a fully horned bison at a Frontiers Day Wild West show in 1910 as an exhibition stunt. He was showing off to President Theodore Roosevelt, who happened to be in the audience.

On rare occasions, bison are ridden as part of local American parades, adding an exotic air to the proceedings. Although a popular sight, there is always a risk that some loud noise may startle them and cause them to bolt, and a stampeding bison is such a powerful force that, if members of the pubic happen to be in the way, there is always a risk of injury. For this reason, the bison has remained little more than a novelty as a beast of burden.

Surprisingly, considering how rare bison-riding is in reality, a feature film appeared in 1978 called *The Buffalo Rider*, in which the hero, finding a bison calf about to be eaten by coyotes, rescues and raises it. He calls the bison Samson and decides to break him like a horse, saddling him and becoming the daring 'Buffalo Rider' of the title. The film is a bizarre disaster and one critic commented wryly, 'Every animal was harmed during the making of this film', but the performances of Samson the bison and his rider are amazing. The understanding between the two is uncanny and, if nothing else, the film demonstrates just how close a rider and his bison can become.

Like most mammals, if hand-raised by humans from birth, bison will stay friendly towards their owners. The problem is not so much whether they will continue to nuzzle gently rather than make a headlong charge, but whether the presence of their huge bulk can be enjoyed without risk to life, limb and furniture at close quarters. One man decided it was worth taking the chance and his relationship with his gigantic household pet is truly remarkable.

Texas Cowboy Ronald Bridges, nicknamed the 'Buffalo Whisperer', was an unusually daring rodeo performer when he

Pet bison Wildthing with Ronald Bridges in his room at home in Quinlan, Texas.

was younger. It was a career that saw him break most of his bones, have his teeth kicked in and his neck broken twice. By comparison, hand-rearing a tame bison looked like child's play and in July 2005 Bridges acquired a two-month old bull bison and started bottle-feeding him. Given the appropriate pet name of Wildthing, the young animal loved coming into the house so much that Bridges eventually gave him a room of his own.

Five years later, in 2010, Wildthing weighed 590 kg (1,300 lb) and in 2014, at the age of nine, had reached the impressive weight of 1,089 kg (2,400 lb). Fortunately he is a gentle giant, remaining docile and friendly and, despite his huge size, is still allowed to enter the house. Amazingly, he never fouls the house, always going outside to relieve himself. His self-control is so remarkable that he is even allowed to go for rides in his owner's pick-up truck. Because the bison is by nature a herding animal, Wildthing hates being alone. This is why he loved entering the house when he was young – to be close to his human family. As an adult, he stays by Bridges's side whenever he can. If the man is working outside the house, the bison follows him everywhere. If Bridges is inside the house, sitting by the window, the bison lies down outside the window, as near to him as possible.

To give Wildthing more company, Bridges acquired a second young bison. Called Bullet, this one was a mere 408-kg (900-lb) female but she soon began to put on weight. As she grew bigger she insisted on accompanying Wildthing inside the house. In estate agent terms, the Bridges dwelling must now be referred to as a Two-bison Home.

Bridges and his wife Sherron, who has Chickasaw, Chocataw and Blackfoot blood in her veins, live at Quinlan, near Dallas, and have become famous as the 'buffalo couple', appearing at local events with their unusual pets. They claim to be the only couple ever to ride in a bison-drawn chariot and made the head-lines when Wildthing acted as best man when they renewed their wedding vows in 2008. He even performed the traditional duty of a best man by presenting the wedding rings, one on the end of each horn.

It would be reasonable to suppose that the relationship between Bridges and his pet bison is unique, but that is not the case. Quite independently, in 2008, a Canadian rancher by the name of Jim Sautner, living in Spruce Grove, near Edmonton, Alberta, acquired an orphaned bison when it was only a few weeks old and began to hand-rear it as a house pet in exactly the same way. Like Wildthing, Sautner's pet bison, called Bailey, is allowed into the house and, again like Wildthing, is gentle and restrained with his human family. He also goes for rides in his owner's car, in this case a converted Pontiac that was specially modified to accommodate his huge frame. Watching him sniffing the air as the car glides along, it is clear that he enjoys this experience in much the same way as a pet dog. When the car stops at a local bar, Bailey has been known to enter the premises and sample the beer. By 2013, when Bailey was five years old, he weighed 826 kg (1,821 lb), heavier than the 590 kg (1,300 lb) that Wildthing weighed at the same age. This suggests that perhaps Bailey is a Canadian wood bison – a big-ger, darker, northern race – and that eventually he will end up as a larger adult than Wildthing, who is almost certainly a southern plains bison.

When these two bulls develop the urge to mate, it will be interesting to discover whether their friendly relations with their human companions manage to survive their sexual maturity. In the wild state this is the time when they would start to feel a deep-seated urge to headbutt rival males and to assert themselves as dominant members of the herd. For the sake of Bridges and

Sautner, one can only hope that this new phase of their fascinating projects passes peacefully and does not end in disaster. Fortunately for Sautner, Bailey clearly sees him not as a rival male but as his mother, because he still sucks on his hand whenever he gets the chance. So, with luck, he will not feel the urge to headbutt Sautner when the mating urge asserts itself. The same will probably be true for Bridges.

BISON IN RODEOS

It is a brave man who is prepared to ride a bucking bison in a rodeo show, but it has been attempted in the past. For those unfamiliar with rodeo techniques, it should be explained that the bucking animals are not reacting so violently because they are wild and unbroken, but because they have been fitted with flank straps that are pulled tight around their abdomens just before the gate is opened and they are let out into the ring. This flank or bucking strap causes them considerable pain and their frantic bucking is simply an attempt to stop this pain. The strap is removed as soon as they have thrown their rider and been rounded up. (It is because of this cruelty that the rodeo is illegal in Britain.)

A close examination of photographs of bison being ridden in rodeos reveals that, in some cases, the animals have been de-horned, to protect the riders from being gored. A more cunning procedure is to remove the true horns and replace them with rubber ones that look real from a distance. In a few cases, however, riders are brave enough to risk riding on horned bison.

BISON IN CIRCUSES

Because of its character – charging when angered, stampeding when panicked – it is clear that the bison is highly unsuited to

life as a circus performer. So it is not surprising to discover that at the present time there is only one solitary bison performing in a circus in front of a closely packed audience of children and adults potentially at risk. That animal is an eight-year-old American bison called Tatanka (which is Cheyenne for bison), a star of the Zerbini Family Circus that tours 100 North American towns annually, bringing an old-fashioned travelling circus to the local communities.

The Zerbinis are one of the oldest circus families in the world and can trace their involvement back through eight generations to 1763. As circus performers they left Europe in 1868 and moved to America, where they eventually started their own circus in 1992. The bison Tatanka was rescued (presumably from the food market) when it was four years old by Alain Zerbini who has trained it to perform a simple act. It is led into the ring and circles while a large see-saw is erected. It then walks up and over this see-saw and ends by taking a bow, lowering itself by bending its front legs. As circus acts go, it is about as simple as it gets, but the audience is always amazed to see such a huge (2,000 lb/900 kg) beast at very close quarters.

With animal performances in circuses coming under fire recently, it is not surprising that voices have been raised against this bison act. TAPS, the Traveling Animal Protection Society, has accused the Zerbini Circus of 'torturing' the bison. The organization FAUN, Friends of Animals United, has described the Zerbini Circus as a 'disgusting caravan of animal abuse'. They add:

> In the wild and in spacious sanctuaries, bison do not walk across a see-saw board, as Tatanka is forced to do. Instead, bison commonly choose to roam, some for miles each day, while grazing on grasses and sedges, a choice Tatanka is denied while confined in trailers and forced to perform on the circus tour.

This is all perfectly true, and it is grossly unnatural for any wild animal to be put through a routine inside the big top of a travelling circus. It would, however, be interesting to know whether, if Tatanka could be given a free choice, it would rather be a bison-burger or an entertainer.

8 Bison Evolution

The ancestor of the two modern bison species, the steppe bison (*Bison priscus*), split off from the other ancient cattle about five million years ago, probably somewhere in northern Asia. Like its close relative, the yak, it was a tough, cold country species, able to withstand the rigours of an icy climate. The most successful of all the early cattle species, it was the only one to spread its range right across the globe, from Western Europe to North America. The steppe bison is well known from fossil skeletons and there is even a deep-frozen specimen that was discovered in Alaska in 1979. Given the nickname 'Blue Babe', it had been so well preserved that it was possible to study its soft tissues as well as its bones.

In Europe, the steppe bison evolved into the modern European bison and was replaced by it about 11,000 years ago. In North America it evolved into the American bison, which replaced it about 8,000 years ago, but there the story was more complicated. What happened was that the steppe bison migrated across what is now the Bering Strait, but which was a land bridge about 500,000 years ago, and entered the continent of North America. There, it was the only cattle species present and, having no rivals and few predators, it flourished. There were three separate waves of bison migration between 500,000 and 220,000 years ago and each of these waves led to the evolution

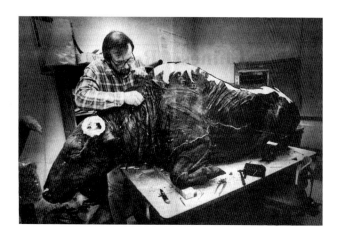

A taxidermist working to restore the once-frozen remains of a steppe bison specimen, known as 'Blue Babe', preserved in permafrost in Alaska.

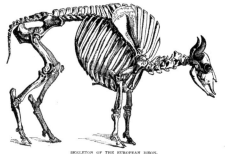

SKELETON OF THE EUROPEAN BISON.

Skeleton of the European bison (*Bison bonasus*).

of a new species in the American environment. The first wave of this intercontinental migration led to the evolution of a species with dramatically enlarged horns, called the giant or longhorn bison, *Bison latifrons*. This huge animal appeared about 500,000 years ago in central North America and survived until the end of the Pleistocene, becoming extinct about 20,000 to 30,000 years ago.

The horn-span of the ancestral steppe bison was only about 120 cm (47 in), whereas the giant bison boasted a horn-span of 213 cm (83 in). The second wave of migration led to the evolution of another species, the thick-horned bison (*Bison crassicornis*), with a horn-span of only 132 cm (52 in.). This was a less successful species, never spreading its range beyond Alaska and northern Canada. The third wave of migration led to the evolution of yet another species, the ancient bison (*Bison antiquus*) about 250,000 years ago. This species had a more modest horn-span of about 86 cm (34 in.) and was extremely successful, ranging from Alaska down to Mexico. This in turn evolved into a transitional species, the western bison (*Bison occidentalis*), the first of the American bison species to have its horns pointing upwards like hooks, and this finally led to the smaller, modern American bison (*Bison bison*) about 5,000 years ago, with the smallest horn-span of all (73 cm; 29 in.).

An archaeologist standing next to a giant bison skull excavated in Colorado gives a sense of scale – note the huge horns!

The skull of the thick-horned bison (*Bison priscus*).

Looking back over the extinct species of bison it is clear that the general evolutionary trend has been to reduce the size and spread of the horns. The successful, modern bison species have their modest horns bent up and neatly tucked into the sides of the head. It is worth considering what the advantage of this horn reduction might be. The horns have two functions – defence against predators such as wolves and defence against rival bison. Films of bison being attacked by wolves reveals that the upward-hooking movement of the bison's head is extremely effective, capable of flinging an impaled wolf high up into the air. In this respect horn reduction seems to have cost nothing in terms of efficiency. The same applies to fights between rival bison. The giant horns of the extinct species, although making an impressive visual display at a distance, would have had the disadvantage of making the animals more cumbersome. Modern bison, as already mentioned, can run for considerable distances at a speed of 35 miles an hour. Over short distances they can even reach 40 miles an hour. If they were carrying huge, heavy, spread-out horns, this would weigh them down and inevitably reduce their speed.

It should be stressed that the dates given for the appearance and disappearance of the various extinct species of bison are only a rough guide. Different authorities give slightly different dates. This is because such dates are always estimates and can never be precise. Even when a particular skull has been accurately dated, this can only tell us that one particular animal was alive at that time. It cannot tell us the date of the appearance or the disappearance of the whole species.

To sum up, the known bison species and subspecies are as follows:

The skeleton of the ancient bison (*Bison antiquus*).

In both Europe and North America:
Bison priscus   Steppe bison

In Europe:
Bison bonasus bonasus   Lowlands bison
Bison bonasus caucasicus   Caucasian bison
Bison bonasus hungarorum   Hungarian bison

In North America:
Bison latifrons   Giant bison
Bison crassicornis   Thick-horned bison
Bison antiquus   Ancient bison
Bison occidentalis   Western bison
Bison bison athabascae   Wood bison
Bison bison bison   Plains bison

9 Bison in Natural History

Anatomically, it has to be said, the bison is very strange. It has been described as an animal with the front half of a mountain gorilla and the rear half of a racehorse. Fanciful as this description is, it is easy enough to see what provoked it. The bison may be built like a gorilla at the front, with its great bulk and its heavy coat of fur, but it can run like the wind and cover the ground at speeds that make nonsense of its seemingly lumbering form.

To understand this contradiction – bulk and speed – it is useless to look at the animal from the side. A frontal view, or a rear one, is necessary. Seen this way a remarkable fact emerges – the apparently massive body of the bison is very narrow. It is as if someone laid it on its side and tried to squash it flat. This is a clever evolutionary trick. It gives the bison a frighteningly impressive silhouette when it is approached from the side but, once it is panicked, it can gallop for considerable distances at 35 miles an hour (56 km/h) because it is so much lighter on its feet than it looks.

The jumping ability of the bison has to be seen to be believed. For such a stocky, seemingly cumbersome animal, its athletic leaping is truly remarkable. This was vividly demonstrated when

nine bison escaped from a farm in Maryland in 2005. The police thought they had them cornered when they herded them into a local tennis court, but to their astonishment the animals leapt the tennis nets with ease to evade them. On other occasions bison have been reported to jump as high as six feet off the ground.

Physically the bison is the most impressive of all the wild cattle. Its unusual build gives it the appearance of an animal of immense power and its permanently lowered head gives the impression that it is always about to charge. Its massive skull, so essential for bulls when they engage in headbutting contests during the mating season, is equipped with a huge, convex forehead and a pair of tightly curved horns. Acting as a shock absorber during the mating battles, there is a large hump of flesh on the shoulders, supported by bony extensions of the backbone. Beneath the jaws of the bull there hangs a big, drooping beard. The coat of coarse brown hair is long and dense all over the head and chest and on the upper parts of the front legs, creating a heavy, matted mane. A fully grown male stands at about 2 metres (6 ½ ft) at the shoulders

American bull bison showing how the thick coat on the front of the body stops abruptly in mid-body.

Despite its massive form the bison has a narrow body when viewed frontally.

The jumping ability of the bison displayed here by a farm escapee.

and can weigh over 900 kg (2,000 lb). The record is 1,133 kg (2,500 lb).

In addition to the obvious differences in shape and build between bison and oxen, there are also two hidden differences in the bony anatomy. Whereas the ox only has thirteen pairs of ribs, the European bison has fourteen and the American has fifteen. The tail of the ox is longer, having 21 vertebrae, while the bison's tail has only nineteen. There is also a more conspicuous tuft of hair at the tip of the bison's tail.

BISON PREDATORS

Before the arrival of man in North America, the bison's main predators were the wolves, but even a large pack of these were usually forced to make do with only the young or the elderly. A mature adult bison could nearly always hold its own against

Starving wolves risk surrounding an adult American bison.

138

even the hungriest wolf pack. Other occasional predators are grizzly bears, brown bears, coyotes and pumas (cougars), but they would only be able to tackle young animals and even then must face the wrath of violently defensive mothers.

Hand-coloured lithograph after George Catlin, *Buffalo Hunt, White Wolves Attacking Buffalo Bull*, 1844.

BISON FEEDING

The feeding behaviour of bison differs between the two species. The European bison is mostly a browser, preferring the leaves, twigs and bark of trees. The American plains bison is essentially a grazer, feeding almost entirely on grasses. The American wood bison is intermediate between the two. An interesting adaptation to this difference is that the browsing bison of Europe is much taller than the grazing bison of the American plains, with its head held higher. In other words, the head of the

leaf-eater is nearer the leaves and the head of the grass-eater is nearer the grass, giving both species a starting advantage when they begin foraging.

In addition to grass, leaves, twigs and bark, bison of both species will occasionally take brushwood or seedling stems. Feeding mostly by day, they will cover an average of approximately 3 kilometres (2 miles) a day in their restless search for food. They could probably eat almost as much while staying put in one place, so there have to be other advantages to their roaming behaviour. Two possibilities are: slowly increasing their knowledge of the topography of their habitat – an asset in an emergency; and moving away from their own droppings as they feed. There is also the need to find water on a daily basis, which will account for part of their group movements.

In the winter, when snow lies deep on the ground, bison can be seen rooting vigorously into it with their muzzles to get at the grasses concealed below. Surprisingly, they do not seem to use their hooves very often during this activity, despite the fact that they are well known to paw the ground when they are readying themselves for a fight.

In addition to their daily wanderings, there are more dramatic seasonal migrations. In the old days, before human interferences, the plains bison of America would migrate several hundred miles in huge herds as winter approached. Then, in the spring, they would head north again. In this way they could avoid the extremes of temperature.

WALLOWING BEHAVIOUR

Like many large herbivores, bison are plagued by clouds of insects hour after hour, especially during the summer. One defence they have is to indulge in vigorous wallowing in dust bowls of their own

When they are required to do so bison can swim for long distances: the Yellowstone River upstream of LeHardy Rapids, September 2001.

American bison in the snow.

making. If there is mud, so much the better, but if not, clouds of dust will help.[1] One strange feature of this wallowing behaviour is that it is done mostly by the bulls, as if there is some kind of display element in it – throwing themselves about as an advertisement, perhaps, of their physical strength. Supporting this idea is the observation that, once one bull has started a wallow, he will soon be displaced by the dominant bull of the group and, when that one has finished, other bulls will follow him, one after the other, until almost all the males have rolled around, kicking their legs in the air and throwing up a cloud of dust that is sometimes so large that it obscures the whole herd. The cows, by comparison, rarely wallow. If pest control were the sole function of wallowing, one would expect the females to do just as much as the males, so there does seem to be some sort of social communication involved.[2]

Bison bull wallowing in dustbowl as a way of ridding itself of insect pests.

So intense is this wallowing behaviour that the dust bowls grow larger as they are used time and again. A typical one will be 60 cm (2 ft) deep and as much as 6 m (20 ft) across. Early settlers were so impressed by them as they travelled across the plains that their diaries make special mention of them. Later, after the terrible bison slaughter, the wallows remained long after the herds had vanished, a sad reminder of what had once been.

George Catlin, writing in the nineteenth century, gives a vivid description of how a new wallow is made:

In the summer these animals suffer greatly from heat, and wherever there is a little stagnant water lying in the grass, and the ground underneath, the enormous bull, lowered down upon one knee, will plunge his horns, and at last his head, driving up the earth, and soon making an excavation in the ground. Into this the water filters from among the grass . . . he throws himself flat upon his side, and forcing himself violently around, with his horns and his huge hump on his shoulders presented to the sides, he ploughs up the ground by his rotary motion, sinking himself deeper and deeper in the ground, continually enlarging his pool, into which he at length becomes nearly immersed. The water and mud about him mixed into a complete mortar, drips in streams from every part of him as he rises up on his feet.[3]

The advantage of mud wallows over dust wallows is that they provide the bison with a thick armour of dried, caked mud that helps to prevent stinging insects from attacking the skin. Body movements will eventually crack this armour and reduce its efficiency, so repeated wallowing may be called for, especially in the heat of summer, providing the animals can find the all-important damp patches in the grass.

In addition to wallowing, bison also relieve skin irritations by rubbing themselves against large stones, rocks or trees. They also roll on the ground from time to time without going to the length of creating a deep wallow. This is often seen in the spring when they are shedding the heavy winter coats, which by now may be hanging in irregular clumps and tatters. Care has to be taken with captive bison because their powerful rubbing actions can cause damage to fences, log structures and posts. An early settler who built his log cabin close to a salt spring was horrified to find that the herds of bison visiting the spring would approach his cabin and start rubbing hard against its log

The remains of a bison wallow photographed in Kansas in 1897.

walls with such vigour that 'In a few hours they *rubbed* the house completely down, taking delight in turning the logs off with their horns, while he had some difficulty to escape from being trampled under their feet or crushed to death in his own ruins.'[4]

The cry of the bison has been described as mostly groans and grunts, instead of the typical lowing sound of domestic cattle. At the start of the breeding season, however, there is a dramatic change in the vocalizations of the bulls. A deep, rumbling roar can now be heard wafting across the plains, heralding the start of the rutting displays. So loud is this call that it can be heard as far as 5 kilometres (3 miles) away. As the aggressive mood grows, several bulls may join in a noisy, bellowing concert. Then the physical challenges begin, with dominant males seeing off new challengers with concussive head-butts.

Before the breeding season the bulls tend to keep to the outskirts of the groups of cows with their growing offspring, but once the headbutting contests have been resolved, the winners move in to be close to the cows. They must now wait until one of the cows is ready to mate. During this phase a strange facial expression can be seen on the face of the rutting bulls, especially when they encounter a cow that is urinating. Called the *flehmen* response, or flaring face, it reveals that the bull is savouring the sexual fragrance of the cow, checking to see if she is ready to mate. During the *flehmen*, the bull curls his upper lip back, exposing his palate. As he does this, he inhales the air deeply and stays like this, holding the expression for several seconds. During these moments the female scents gain access to a duct just inside the roof of the bull's mouth. This duct leads to the vomero-nasal

During the rutting season the adult males engage in violent headbutting.

The *flehmen* response of the bull during courtship.

organ where the airborne odours are examined for clues as to the sexual condition of the cow. If these clues reveal that she is receptive and ready to mate, the bull will make his move and mount her.

The mating season runs from June until September, with the peak of mating activity occurring in July and August. The cows have a nine-month pregnancy and most of the calves are born in April or May the following year, although some are born later. The birth is very quick and the vulnerable newborn can walk within an hour and run with the herd within one day. Amazingly, some precocious calves have been seen to run with the herd when they are only three hours old. Typically, each cow has a single calf, weighing between 18 and 32 kg (40 and 70 lb) at birth. At first, the coat is a much lighter colour than that of

The bison calf can walk, even run, within one day of its birth.

the adult, but it soon begins to darken, a yearling's coat being as dark as its mother's. The back of the newborn lacks the adult hump, but this starts to grow when the animal is only a few months old. The period of time that the calves feed from their mothers varies a great deal, some starting to graze very early, while others continue to take milk for months. This variation depends to some extent on the temperament of the mother.

The young bison will stay close to their mothers in the female herd until they are about three years old. After this, if they are males, they will start to move out and join the older males. They will reach maturity when they are between seven and eight years old. In the wild they can hope to live to an age of at least twenty years and often up to 30. In captivity, where they are protected, the life span can reach as much as 40 years. The cows are capable of producing one calf a year for the whole of their adult lives.

Finally, there is one special kind of bison that demands attention, and that is the extremely rare white bison. Zoologically, it could be ignored as a minor oddity but it deserves a brief mention because it has become a favourite subject of American Indian folklore and an entire film has been based on its mythical status.

Usually referred to as the White Buffalo, this form can be of four types. First is the full albino, completely lacking in pigment, with pure white fur and pink eyes. Second is the leucistic, with white fur and blue eyes. Third is a rare condition that creates a white calf but with the fur turning to brown within the first two years of its life. And fourth, there are occasional hybrids with white domestic cattle that are born white, or partly white, because they are not pure-bred animals. The true albino bison is so uncommon that it has been estimated to appear only once in every ten million births. Little wonder then that it has been so revered in the past.

American Indian tribes have always considered a white buffalo to be sacred or, at the very least, possessed of special spiritual powers. They offer prayers to it and perform rituals in its honour. In the popular tribal legend of the White Buffalo Calf Woman, the white buffalo appears in the form of a beautiful young woman wearing white hides. She teaches the tribe various ceremonial practices including how to smoke the pipe of peace and perform sacred music. She promises that, when she returns, she will bring peace and prosperity. In their darkest hours, Native Indian tribes

Big Medicine, a white bison that lived from 1933 to 1959 on the National Bison Range and is now on permanent display at the Montana Historical Society, St Helena.

The White Buffalo film poster.

clung to the hope that she would reappear and bring an end to their suffering.

In 1994 a white bison calf was born on a farm near Janesville in Wisconsin. As a ten-million-to-one chance, she was given the appropriate name of Miracle, and was reputedly the first white calf born since 1933. She was seen as a sign of hope by American Indians and was visited on her farm by many admirers, some of whom offered up prayers in her presence. To believers she was seen as a sign that White Buffalo Calf Woman was returning to fulfil a sacred prophesy and that she would 'bring back spiritual balance and harmony'. In 2001 Chief Arvol Looking Horse, Nineteenth Generation Keeper of the Sacred White Buffalo Calf Pipe, issued a formal statement in which he declared that

Charging...Roaring...Breathing Fire and Hell...
THE WHITE EARTHQUAKE IS HERE!

YOU WON'T BELIEVE YOUR EYES!

CHARLES BRONSON
"THE WHITE BUFFALO"

DINO DE LAURENTIIS presents

CHARLES BRONSON in "THE WHITE BUFFALO" starring JACK WARDEN · WILL SAMPSON

also starring CLINT WALKER · SLIM PICKENS · STUART WHITMAN · and KIM NOVAK as 'Poker Jenny'

Screenplay by RICHARD SALE, from his novel "The White Buffalo" · Directed by J. LEE THOMPSON · Produced by PANCHO KOHNER

Music by JOHN BARRY

United Artists
A Transamerica Company

77/88

"THE WHITE BUFFALO"

We have a prophecy . . . that someday the spirit of the White Buffalo Calf Woman would stand upon Mother Earth. At that time, great changes would happen to Mother Earth . . . We ask the people of the Global Community to pray with us for global healing.

Sadly, Miracle was a disappointment on two counts: her white coat had turned brown by the time she was an adult and she died unexpectedly at the age of ten. Her early death and the loss of her sacred white coat should have robbed her of her spiritual status, but the faithful had invested too much hope in her to abandon her. Prayers were offered up at her grave and a large white statue of her in the guise of the White Buffalo Calf Woman still stands at the entrance to the farm where she lived out her short life.

The extreme rarity of white bison calves has always been an important factor in endowing them with their spiritual qualities. One was recorded in 1833, another in 1876 and a third in 1933. Then there was a 60-year wait until Miracle arrived in 1994. So it is little wonder that she caused such a stir. Since then, however, the picture has changed in a remarkable way, because between 1997 and 2012 no fewer than 26 white calves were recorded. The Spirit Mountain Ranch alone had a herd of fifteen of these. This means that either the white mutation has never been particularly rare, and that poor records were kept in earlier times when compared with today, or alternatively that the mutation rate has increased dramatically in recent years for some unknown, genetic reason. Geneticists have been studying the phenomenon and are wondering whether the increase could be due to exposure to some new kind of chemical or radiation factor. A more likely explanation is that, at some point in the past, crosses were made between bison and white cattle and that this genetic contamination of pure-bred bison stock was forgotten about as animals were moved from ranch to ranch.

The Lakota Indians have a more spiritual explanation. They see the dramatic rise in the number of white calves as a sign that, in our modern, troubled times, there is an increased need for people to unify and settle their differences.

Bison on the road to recovery.

Appendix 1: Bison in Films

1926   *Buffalo Bill on the u.p. Trail*, dir. Frank S. Mattison (western)

1931   *Battling with Buffalo Bill*, dir. Ray Taylor (12-episode serial)

1933   *The Thundering Herd*, dir. Henry Hathaway (western), starring Randolph Scott

1944   *Buffalo Bill*, dir. William Wellman (western), starring Joel McCrea and Maureen O'Hara

1947   *Buffalo Bill Rides Again*, dir. Bernard B. Ray (western)

1952   *Buffalo Bill in Tomahawk Territory*, dir. Bernard B. Ray (western)

1962   *Buffalo Gun*, dir. Albert C. Gannaway (western)

1964   *Buffalo Bill*, dir. Mario Costa (western), starring Gordon Scott

1976   *Buffalo Bill and the Indians*, dir. Robert Altman (western), starring Paul Newman

1977   *The White Buffalo*, dir. J. Lee Thompson (western), starring Charles Bronson

1978   *Buffalo Rider*, dir. John Fabian, starring Rick Guinn

1990   *Dances with Wolves*, dir. and starring Kevin Costner

1995   *Buffalo Girls*, dir. Ron Hardy (western), starring Angelica Huston, Melanie Griffith and Jack Palance

1997   *Buffalo Soldiers*, dir. Charles Haid (western)

2010   *Facing the Storm: Story of the American Bison*, dir. Doug Hawes-Davis (documentary)

2012   *Buffalo Bill et la conquête de l'Ouest*, dir. Vincent Froehly (documentary)

Appendix 2: Close Relatives of the Bison

The two bison species have ten close relatives that, with them, make up the Tribe Bovini – the Wild Cattle. They are as follows:

Genus BUBALUS	THE ASIATIC BUFFALOES	
1 *Bubalus bubalis*	WATER BUFFALO	India, Nepal, Burma, Indochina, Malaysia
2 *Bubalus depressicornis*	LOWLAND ANOA	Celebes (Sulawesi) lowlands
3 *Bubalus quarlesi*	MOUNTAIN ANOA	Celebes (Sulawesi) mountains
4 *Bubalus mindorensis*	TAMARAW	Philippines (Mindoro)
Genus BOS	THE TRUE CATTLE	
5 *Bos javanicus*	BANTENG	Burma, Java, Borneo, Indochina, Bali
Bos banten	BALI CATTLE (Domestic)	
6 *Bos gaurus*	GAUR	India, Malaysia, Burma, Indochina
Bos frontalis	GAYAL (Domestic)	
7 *Bos sauveli*	KOUPREY	Indochina
8 *Bos mutus*	YAK	Tibet
Bos grunniens	YAK (Domestic)	
9 *Bos primigenius*	AUROCHS	Europe, W. Asia
Bos taurus	OX (Domestic)	
Bos indicus	ZEBU (Domestic)	

Genus SYNCEROS	AFRICAN BUFFALO	
10 *Synceros caffer*	AFRICAN BUFFALO	Africa

Genus BISON	BISON	
11 *Bison bison*	AMERICAN BISON (BUFFALO)	North America
12 *Bison bonasus*	EUROPEAN BISON (WISENT)	Eastern Europe

Today some of these species are extremely rare in the wild and two of them have become extinct in the last few centuries. Five of them have been domesticated. The world populations, both wild and domestic, have been estimated as follows:

SPECIES	WILD POPULATION	DOMESTIC POPULATION
1 WATER BUFFALO	3,400	172 million
2 LOWLAND ANOA	less than 5,000	none
3 MOUNTAIN ANOA	less than 2,500	none
4 TAMARAW	263 in 2008	none
5 BANTENG	5,000–8,000	1.5 million
6 GAUR	13,000–30,000	100,000 in 1968
7 KOUPREY	few dozen	none
8 YAK	10,000	12 million
9 AUROCHS	none since 1627	1.3 billion
10 AFRICAN BUFFALO	just under 1 million	none
11 AMERICAN BISON	15,000 (released)	515,000 (ranches & reserves)
12 EUROPEAN BISON	1,790 (released)	1,410 (parks & reserves)

This is not the place to discuss the close relatives of the bison in any detail, but a brief portrait of each of the ten species is helpful, to set the bison in their evolutionary position.

Water buffalo
(*Bubalus bubalis*).

1 WATER BUFFALO

As it exists today the Asian water buffalo is virtually a domestic species. Unlike the aurochs, however, where the wild form is completely extinct, there still remains a small wild population living in India, Nepal, Bhutan, Thailand and possibly Burma. Until recently there were also small populations surviving in Pakistan, Bangladesh, Laos and Vietnam, but these are now extinct. At the last count there was a global total of only 3,400 wild water buffalo, 3,100 of which were living in India. Compared with the 172 million domesticated water buffalo, this is a trivial 0.002 per cent of the world population of this species. Of the domestic animals, there are 98 million in India, over 23 million in Pakistan, nearly 23 million in China and over one million in Thailand. There are also large populations in South America and Australia and even some in Europe. The wild form is slightly larger than the domesticated version and more aggressive. The only natural predator they fear is the tiger. The short coat is a dull black and the curved, ridged horns are massive – the largest of all the wild cattle species. They also have the longest gestation period – ten to eleven months compared with the bison's nine months. As their name suggests, this species spends a great deal of time wallowing in shallow water and is never far from it. This helps to keep it cool and to rid it of troublesome insect pests. The herds are small, rarely exceeding 30 animals.

2 LOWLAND ANOA

The lowland anoa, also known as the midget buffalo, is a small, island-dwelling relative of the Asian water buffalo. It is found only in Indonesia, where it is restricted to two islands, the larger Celebes (Sulawesi) and the smaller Buton Island off its

Lowland anoa (*Bubalus depressicornis*).

southeast coast. The sharply pointed horns, with a triangular cross section, point backwards without any curl. The dull black coat shows a few very small white markings, especially on the side of the head and the lower legs. It is the least sociable of all the wild cattle and frequently lives an almost solitary life, browsing on the forest vegetation. The expansion of human settlements on the islands is starting to take its toll on this species and its future looks bleak. Making matters worse is the fact that local hunters have no other large game to preoccupy them and so, despite all attempts at protection, the last remaining wild anoa are being shot and their numbers are falling dramatically year by year. It may be illegal to kill them according to Indonesian law, but it is still possible to buy their meat in the local markets.

3 MOUNTAIN ANOA

Like its close relative, the lowland anoa, this species is found only in Indonesia, on Celebes (Sulawesi) and Buton Island. The mountain anoa is the smallest of all the wild cattle, standing at no more than 70 cm (28 in) at the shoulder. In fact it is so small that, when encountered, it is sometimes thought to be a deer rather than a member of the cattle tribe. It has a slightly longer coat than the lowland anoa and is generally browner in colour. When it moults its thicker coat between February and April, small white markings are revealed on its head, neck and legs. The single young are born with a much paler brown coat. The horns are modest and point backwards without any curl; in section they are round, unlike those of the closely related lowland anoa which are triangular. Little is known about its behaviour but it is thought to live in pairs and only gathers in small herds at certain times of the year. It is a rainforest dweller, preferring

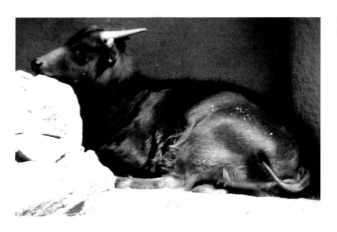

Mountain anoa
(*Bubalus quarlesi*).

locations with easy access to water, where it often wallows and bathes. It has no natural predators apart from man.

4 TAMARAW

The tamaraw, or tamarou, is a dwarf buffalo found only on the island of Mindoro in the Philippines. It is likely that in the past it had a wider range, including other islands in the Philippine archipelago, but in recent times it became restricted to just this one island, which measures about 160 x 80 kilometres (100 x 50 miles). Up until the end of the nineteenth century, malaria prevented humans from settling on Mindoro and the tamaraw occupied most of the island. It is estimated that at that time there were about 10,000 of them living there. Then new anti-malarial drugs allowed human occupation and during the twentieth century the range and numbers of the tamaraw declined rapidly. By the middle of that century, in 1949, the tamaraw population had dropped to 1,000 animals. Within a few years, by 1957, a field study revealed that there were only 244 of these dwarf

Tamaraw (*Bubalus mindorensis*).

buffalos, living in nineteen herds. By 1969 there were less than 100 of them and it looked as though they were about to become extinct. Luckily this was prevented and by 1975 the population had started to increase. There were now 120 of them and by 2008 this figure had risen to 263. Today, with the human population of Mindoro proliferating to over one million people, and with over 470 tourist hotels, the animal is confined to only a few remote grassy plains. Happily, although it is barely surviving, it is still with us and is at last receiving some protection from conservationists. Its future, however, remains uncertain and there are none in captivity to act as backup. In appearance, it is an all-black animal with sturdy, broad, ridged, backward-pointing horns. It used to be diurnal but has become increasingly nocturnal and reclusive since the human invasion of its island. Local people insist that, when threatened with danger, a tamaraw mother will reach down underneath her calf and, using her horns, will gently scoop it up and place it on her back before she gallops away to safety. This is a curious tale to have invented but it seems unlikely to be true.

5 BANTENG

The banteng of South East Asia is the most attractively marked of all the wild cattle. It has a short chestnut coat, usually darker in the bull than the cow, with conspicuous white markings on its lower legs, its rump, above its eyes and on its muzzle. Compared with other wild cattle, its head is rather small, as is its hump, which is little more than a back-ridge. Today this species is found in seven Asiatic countries – Burma, Thailand, Cambodia, Laos, Vietnam, Malaysia and Indonesia – though nowhere in large numbers in the wild state. The total world population is thought to be only a few thousand. On the Island of Java there are now only about 400 surviving; on Sumatra they have all vanished; on Borneo, the Dayak

Banteng (*Bos javanicus*) in a Munich zoo.

head-hunters, now forbidden to collect human heads, collect banteng heads instead. This is a wary animal and its characteristic shyness has led to it becoming nocturnal in areas where there has been human intrusion. On the islands of Bali and Java, the wild banteng were caught and domesticated several centuries ago. The domestic banteng are smaller than the wild ones and are known locally as Bali cattle. They are found today all through Indonesia and are used as beasts of burden and also for their meat. Some were also taken to northern Australia where there are now feral herds.

6 GAUR

The gaur of southern Asia is the largest of the wild oxen and, with its enormous hump, may stand at over 220 cm (7 ft) tall. In its natural habitat only the elephant and the rhino are heavier. With its pale lower legs, its brown-black body and its heavy horns, it is an impressive sight and has often been treated with respect by local people, although it has also been seen as a special challenge to big-game hunters. Because of hunting and loss of habitat it is now considered a rare species, although it is difficult to calculate its exact numbers. Originally it covered a huge range that included forested regions in India, Bangladesh, Bhutan, Nepal, Western China, Burma, Malaysia, Thailand, Vietnam, Cambodia and Laos. Today it survives only in small fragments of this range. The herds are unusually small, varying between eight and 26 individuals. Predation is heavy and the herd has evolved several special responses to attacks by enemies. They create a defensive kindergarten of calves that is constantly surrounded by a ring of aggressive cows. This arrangement stays in place even when the herd is on the move and the cows are always on the lookout for a lurking big cat or other predator. If one of the cows spots something suspicious it gives the alarm call – a soft snort – that alerts the rest of the herd. The snorter also points her head in the direction of the perceived danger, and the others can then focus on this spot. In this way the whole herd is quickly on the defense. There may be one special cow on lookout duty. She keeps her head up, scanning the undergrowth for signs of danger, while the others have their heads down, feeding. If a predator, such as a tiger, starts to attack it is usually a mature bull gaur that confronts it. Uniquely among wild oxen, the gaur does not meet its enemy head-on, but presents itself sideways to the advancing attacker. This is a visual display, showing off the animal's huge bulk in an attempt to make the attacker think twice. It also places the gaur in a position where it is ready to strike sideways with its heavy horns, and many a tiger will have regretted taking on such a formidable opponent. Even so, it has been calculated that about half the calves are lost to predators before they

Gaur (*Bos gaurus*).

reach adulthood. During the mating season the huge bulls join the herds and their mating cries are so spectacular that they can be heard almost a mile away. They are unlike the calls of any other wild oxen, consisting of a long drawn-out 'e-e-e-e' sound rising to a bellowing 'a-oo-uu'. There is a domesticated version of the gaur, called the gayal or mithan, which is smaller than its wild counterpart.

7 KOUPREY

The kouprey, amazingly, was not discovered until 1937. Today it is the rarest of all the wild oxen and some authorities have suggested that there may be no more than a few dozen left in the wild. In fact nobody has seen one since 1988 and there are some zoologists who believe it may already be extinct. What is worse, there are none in zoos or animal parks to act as a backup. The last captive one, a solitary cow, died in Paris Zoo during the Second World War. This extreme rarity and possible extinction is extremely recent. When the species was first discovered in 1937 it was estimated that there were about 2,000 of them. By 1940 the world population had sunk rapidly to 1,000. A 1957 field study put the figure lower still, at between 650 and 850 animals. At the time they were living secretively in the broken forests of northern Cambodia, with a small number also in western Vietnam, eastern Thailand and southern Laos. Later, in 1969, the figure had dropped alarmingly to about 100. Then, in the second half of the twentieth century, the natural habitat of the animal saw devastating destruction from human warfare and political upheaval and this drove down the numbers of surviving kouprey even further. Hungry soldiers and starving refugees are not the world's greatest conservationists. Today this species exists only in the more remote parts of Cambodia –

if it exists at all. In personality they are said to be unusually shy and retiring, which offers a ray of hope for their survival.

In appearance, the kouprey is similar to the gaur, with pale lower legs, a black-brown body and a tall hump. A unique feature of the species, however, concerns the horns of the bulls. These fray conspicuously, creating a 'horn-fringe' just below the horn-tips. Similar fringes occur briefly in other species, but there the horn is soon worn smooth. In the case of the kouprey, this cannot happen because of the sharp curvature of the horns.

8 YAK

The yak, once described as a cow wearing a long skirt, is thought to be the closest relative of the bison. It inhabits the treeless desert steppes of northern Tibet. Its conspicuous, protective skirt of

A domesticated yak (*Bos grunniens*) in Alpine pasture in Austria.

long hairs hangs down from the lower part of the shoulders, from the chest, the upper part of the legs, the flanks and the rear of the animal. The yak is one of the hardiest of all the wild cattle, spending much of the year in snowy landscapes at high altitudes. The females and their young may form very large herds, but the adult males remain solitary or in small groups around the periphery. The bulls only join the main herd at mating time, when there are violent clashes between them as they fight for mating rights, uttering a characteristic grunting sound. In the 1980s it was estimated that there were only a few hundred wild yak still remaining, but this figure has happily proved to be wrong.

Since then several large and hitherto unknown wild populations have been discovered in very remote regions, so that it can now be said that they number not in the hundreds but in the thousands. The yak has been domesticated for many centuries and today the domestic animals far outnumber their wild counterparts. The wild ones may be in their thousands, but the domestic ones are in their millions.

9 AUROCHS

The aurochs is extinct, so if you are shown a photograph of one, what you are seeing is a re-constituted animal, carefully bred back from domestic cattle in an attempt to recreate the original look of the species. The aurochs is the wild ancestor of all domestic cattle. It once occupied a huge range including most of Europe, North Africa and the Middle East. As one of the main sources of meat for early human tribes, it eventually began to decline in numbers. As human populations grew, those of the aurochs shrank, until in early historical times it began to disappear from large regions of its original range. Forest clearing

A copy of a painting from life said to be of the extinct aurochs (*Bos primigenius*).

for farming was the main cause of its decline in western and central Europe, where it was extinct by the fifteenth century. It managed to survive longer in Eastern Europe where the extensive woodlands offered the herds some protection. Even there, however, it did not last much longer. By the sixteenth century hunting had reduced its numbers to just a few and these were kept in a game reserve where they were carefully protected. We know from the records kept at the time that by 1564 there were only 38 left – eleven bulls, 22 cows and five calves. In 1599 the total number had fallen to 24 and the species was hanging on by a thread. In 1602 there were only four of these remaining and the end was close. In 1627 there was only one, a cow that died in that year and brought the once common and highly successful species to a final end.

Despite their disappearance, we know with reasonable accuracy what they looked like. From the skilful cave paintings in France, from old drawings, paintings and verbal descriptions, and from skeletal remains, it was possible to put together a clear image of their appearance. From this, it was possible to initiate a breeding programme in the twentieth century to re-create them. In the 1920s the German brothers Lutz and Heinz Heck started crossing various types of domestic cattle to produce a 'modern aurochs'. They succeeded in recreating an animal that looked very similar but it was not, of course, a true aurochs. It was no more than a cleverly reconstituted 'lookalike'. The Hecks were attacked for suggesting that the aurochs was reborn, but their efforts should not be belittled because they gave us the chance to see what this important species had once looked like. It was, after all, the ancestor of the more than one billion domestic cattle that are alive today, and even in a genetically 'fake' form it is fascinating for us to be able to stare at it and contemplate that it was this animal that virtually gave us modern civilization, allowing us to switch from a primeval hunter-gatherer way of life to the culture of modern farming.

The extinction of the aurochs paralleled that of the European bison and it is interesting to ask why when one of these two species became domesticated the other did not. The answer seems to be that the first efforts at domestication occurred in regions where bison were absent and only the aurochs was commonly encountered. Once the process had begun it would quickly become refined and the modified cattle, selectively bred for docility, would soon become so established that there would be no point in going through the same difficult early stages of 'taming' with the bison species.

10 AFRICAN BUFFALO

The African buffalo is found all over the African continent south of the Sahara. Its short brown coat is so dark that it appears almost black. The special feature of this species is the large boss on the head of the bulls. This shield is formed by the joining of the two deeply curved horns. The drooping ears are large and fringed with hairs. Its ideal habitat offers three key elements: grass, water and cover. It never migrates, but instead moves slowly around a large home range, revisiting its favourite resting places, pastures, watering holes and salt licks. It may keep moving for up to eighteen hours a day, with about ten hours spent grazing. Because of the often intense heat of the environment, regular drinking is vitally important and usually takes place each day at dawn and dusk. Most of the grazing occurs in the late afternoon and in the hours of darkness. During the hottest part of the day they spend most of their time resting and ruminating. The African buffalo tends to rest in the open unless the heat is excessive, in which case it retreats to

African buffalo.

dense cover. The herd size varies considerably from about 50 animals up to several hundred. Where they live in more densely forested regions the groups are much smaller, with herds normally of less than twenty individuals. Socially the herds consist of females and their young with bachelor groups nearby. Older males commonly live apart from the herd except when mating and there is fierce competition between them for females. These males perform threat displays to one another with vigorous head-tossing and if this does not settle matters they resort to serious headbutting. The African buffalo breeds throughout the year, but with a preference for the rainy seasons. A single calf is born after a gestation period of 340 days. The young males stay with their mothers for two years, the young females for much longer. Although in many regions the numbers of African buffalo have fallen dramatically in recent years, it is still a common species.

Appendix 3: Bison Hybrids

Several experiments have been carried out to see what kind of animal could be created by crossing bison with domestic cattle. The challenge was to see if improvements in the quality or quantity of beef could be achieved, or perhaps a greater resistance to extremes of temperature. A weakness is that there is considerable variability in the form of the hybrids.

In North America, a downside of the existence of these hybrids is that they are beginning to infiltrate the wild herds and reduce the numbers of pure-bred American bison.

THE CATTALO

The earliest of these breeding projects was begun in 1894 at Bobcaygeon in Ontario. The Canadian farmer involved wanted, as he put it, to give a cow the fur and hump of a bison. He did produce a herd of hybrids but, when he died in 1912, his animals were dispersed and later breeding attempts that were made with a few of them failed to produce healthy offspring.

Later, in the 1950s, experimental breedings at Manyberries, Alberta, did prove successful is creating crosses that were better protected from the severe cold of the Canadian winters. Their thicker, heavier coats gave them an advantage in foraging. The cattalo crosses were made using a domestic bull and a bison cow. The male offspring were nearly always infertile, but the females were able to produce viable calves. Despite this success, the whole project was abandoned in the 1960s.

THE BEEFALO

In the 1980s the American Beefalo World Registry was established in Kentucky, bringing together under one banner a variety of scattered hybrid breeding programmes from the United States, Canada, Mexico and elsewhere. The goal was to produce a fertile cross using beef cattle and bison. The ratio involved was five parts cattle to three parts bison and there was some considerable success. The crosses were fertile and had several advantages over the ordinary beef cattle.

- They were better at foraging and accepting more roughage in their diet
- Like bison, they were better at coping with extremes of heat and cold
- Their meat was leaner, higher in protein and lower in cholesterol
- The hybrid bulls grew at a faster rate and achieved a larger adult size
- They had a longer productive life
- They were more resistant to disease

Given these advantages, one would imagine a rapidly increased popularity in beefalo production, but this did not happen. The cause seems to have been repeated arguments and disagreements between individual hybrid-breeders, with the result that major beef producers were reluctant to take the risk of getting involved. With more careful and cooperative control of the various breeding schedules, the future may yet see a valuable injection of bison blood into the world of commercial beef production.

THE AMERICAN BREED

In New Mexico in the middle of the twentieth century, a local rancher created a hybrid that was a cross between zebu, traditional domestic cattle and bison, in a ratio of four parts zebu, three parts cattle and one part bison. His aim was to keep infertility problems at a minimum by using only one-eighth of bison blood in his crosses.

THE YAKALO

This is a cross between a yak and an American bison. Technically these hybrids are classified as 'wild animals' and it requires a special permit to own them. Despite this, their popularity is said to be growing because their meat is leaner than that of ordinary domestic cattle.

THE ZUBRON

The Zubron is a cross between a European bison and a domestic cow. As with other 50/50 crosses between bison and domestic cattle, there have been fertility problems. The male offspring are infertile and further breeding has to be done using only the females. If these are mated with either bison bulls or cattle bulls they then produce fertile offspring of either sex. Experiments with this breed began as early as the nineteenth century but were largely abandoned by the 1980s. The aim to produce a healthier breed of cattle seems to have been outweighed by the uncertainties over fertility levels.

Timeline of the Bison

15–25,000 BC	8th century AD	15th century	16th century
Many bison appear in the cave art of France and northern Spain.	Bison start to disappear from western Europe	Urban development in Europe and the clearing of the land for farming reduces the bison's habitat dramatically and its population declines everywhere	An estimated 60 million bison are living in North America

1872	1874	1883	1884
5,000 American bison are killed each day, every day of the year, as 10,000 hunters pour onto the American Plains and bison hunting becomes a popular sport among the rich	Auctions in Texas selling 200,000 American bison hides every few days	Slaughter of the great northern herd of American bison now almost complete	Only 325 wild bison left in the entire USA – including 25 in Yellowstone National Park where they are protected

1919	1923	1927
Thanks to a new respect for the animals, the total population of American bison has risen to 12,521	54 European bison survive in zoos. The Society for the Protection of European Bison is formed	The last free-living European bison is killed and the species is now extinct in the wild

| 1795 | 1840s | 1862 | 1860s |

Russia gains control of Poland's bison forests and the tsar protects the herds to provide hunting for the Russian nobility

American bison living west of the Rocky Mountains have all been exterminated

Rebellion in the Bialowieza region of Poland reduces the European bison herd to 875 animals

Railroads built across the Great Plains divide the American bison into southern and northern herds. Buffalo Bill Cody becomes a famous figure during this decade

| 1889 | 1902 | 1910 | 1918 |

European bison population declines to 380 animals

Now about 700 American bison in private herds and 23 in Yellowstone National Park

Thanks to controlled breeding, there are now 1,032 bison in the u.s. and 1,076 in Canada

At the end of the First World War, retreating German soldiers shoot all but nine surviving European bison

| 1932 | 1960 | 2000 |

Poland declares 11,000 acres of Białowieża Forest as a national park, giving the European bison a safe habitat

31 European bison now exist in the wild, having been reintroduced following a captive breeding programme.

At least 250,000 American bison are now in private herds, many being raised for meat production. Native Americans are reintroducing bison to their tribal lands

References

1 PREHISTORIC BISON

1 P. A. Leason, 'A New View of the Western European Group of
  Quaternary Cave Art', *Proceedings of the Prehistoric Society*, vol. v,
  part 1 (1939), pp. 51–60.
2 Abbé H. Breuil, *Four Hundred Centuries of Cave Art* (Montignac,
  1952).
3 Jean Clottes, ed., 'Newsletter on Rock Art', *Inora*, 29 (2001).
4 Marija Gimbutas, Th*e Language of the Goddess* (London, 1989).
5 Selwyn Dewdney and Kenneth E. Kidd, *Indian Rock Paintings of
  the Great Lakes* (Toronto, 1962).
6 Ibid.
7 Ekkehart Malotki and Henry Wallace, 'Columbian Mammoth
  Petroglyphs from the San Juan River Near Bluff, Utah, United
  States', *Rock Art Research*, XXVIII/2 (2001), pp. 143–52.
8 Ibid.

2 BISON IN EUROPEAN HISTORY

1 Daniel P. Mannix, *Those About to Die* (New York, 1958).
2 *Heimskringla*, the Old Norse kings' saga was written in Old
  Norse in Iceland by the poet and historian Snorri Sturluson
  around AD 1230. Olaf the Saint's Saga is the longest, the most
  important and the most complete of all the sagas in the
  Heimskringla.

3 E. S. Brooks, *Historic Boys* (London, 1900).

4 Robert Wilde (About.com European History) Roberta Frank, 'The Invention of the Viking Horned Helmet', *International Scandinavian and Medieval Studies in Memory of Gerd Wolfgang Weber* (2000).

5 Pliny, *The Historie of the World: commonly called, the Naturall Historie of C. Plinius Secondus*, trans. Philemon Holland (London, 1635). Quotation from: The first Tome, 8th Book, Chapter xv, p. 200.

6 T. H. White, *The Book of Beasts* (London, 1954), p. 33. This book is a translation of a twelfth-century Bestiary in the Cambridge University Library.

7 Francisco Lopez de Gomara, *La Historia General de las Indias* (Saragossa, 1553; Antwerp, 1554).

8 Edward Topsel, *The History of Four-footed Beasts and Serpents* (London, 1658).

9 Ulyssis Aldrovandi, *Quadrupedum omnium bisulcorum historia* (Bologna, 1642).

10 Johannes Jonstonus, *Historiae Naturalis* (Amsterdam, 1657).

11 Charles F. Partington, ed., *The British Cyclopaedia of Natural History* (London, 1835).

3 BISON IN AMERICAN HISTORY

1 Joe Ben Wheat, 'A Paleo-Indian Bison Kill', *Scientific American*, ccxvi/1 (1967), pp. 44–53.

2 Mark Twain, 'The Noble Red Man', in *The Galaxy* (1870).

3 Delaney P. Boyd, *Conservation of North American Bison: Status and Recommendations* (Calgary, AB, 2003).

4 Deborah Epstein Popper and Frank J. Popper, 'The Great Plains: From Dust to Dust', *Planning* (December 1987).

6 BISON AS A VISUAL IMAGE

1 Colin Eisler, *Dürer's Animals* (Washington, DC, 1991), pp. 100–101, pl. 4.14.

2 Ibid., pp. 53–4, pl. 2.24; p. 102, pl. 4.15.
3 Edgar William Paxson, *E. S. Paxson, Frontier Artist* (Boulder, CO, 1984).

7 BISON AS COMPANIONS

1 J.M.C. Toynbee, *Animals in Roman Life and Art* (London, 1973).
2 Mikolaj Hussowski, *Carmen de statura, feritate ac venatione bisontis* ('A Song about the Appearance, Savagery and Hunting of the Bison') (Kraków, 1523).
3 Antonio De Solis, *History of the Conquest of Mexico by the Spaniards* (London, 1724).
4 Chalmers P. Mitchell, *Centenary History of the Zoological Society of London* (London, 1929), pp. 247–9.

9 BISON IN NATURAL HISTORY

1 Bryan R. Coppedge and James H. Shaw, 'American bison *Bison bison* wallowing behavior and wallow formation on tallgrass prairie', *Acta Theriologica*, XLV/1 (2000), pp. 103–10.
2 Brock R. McMillan, Michael R Cottam and Donald W. Kaufman, 'Wallowing Behavior of American Bison (Bos Bison) in Tallgrass Prairie: an Examination of Alternate Explanations', *American Midland Nauralist.*, 111 (2000), pp. 159–67.
3 George Catlin, *My Life Among the Indians* (New York, 1915), chapter XXI, p. 228.
4 Thomas Ashe, *Travels in America* (London, 1808).

Select Bibliography

Ahrens, Theodor G., 'The Present Status of the European Bison or
    Wisent', *Journal of Mammalogy*, II (1921), pp. 58–62
Aldrovandi, Ulyssis, *Quadrupedum omnium bisulcorum historia*
    (Bologna, 1642)
Ashe, Thomas, *Travels in America* (London, 1808)
Bailey, James A., *American Plains Bison: Rewilding an Icon* (Helena,
    MT, 2013)
Baille-Grohman, William A., *Sport in Art* (London, 1919)
Bement, Leland C. and Brian J. Carter, *Bison Hunting at Cooper Site:
    Where Lightning Bolts Drew Thundering Herds* (Norman, OK, 1999)
Berman, Ruth, *American Bison* (Minneapolis, MN, 2008)
Bjorklund, Lorence F., *The Bison: The Great American Buffalo*
    (New York, 1970)
Bodden, Valerie, *Amazing Animals: Bison* (Mankato, MT, 2013)
Boyd, Delaney P., *Conservation of North American Bison: Status and
    Recommendations* (Calgary, AB, 2003)
Breuil, Abbé H., *Four Hundred Centuries of Cave Art* (Montignac, 1952)
Brooks, E. S., *Historic Boys* (London, 1900)
Catlin, George, *My Life Among the Indians* (New York, 1915)
Clottes, Jean, ed., 'Newsletter on Rock Art', *Inora*, 29 (2001)
Danz, Harold P., *Of Bison and Man* (Boulder, CO, 1997)
De Solis, Antonio, *History of the Conquest of Mexico by the Spaniards*
    (London, 1724)
Dewdney, Selwyn and Kenneth E. Kidd, *Indian Rock Paintings of the
    Great Lakes* (Toronto, 1962)

Eisler, Colin, *Dürer's Animals* (Washington, DC, 1991)

Fitzgerald, David, *Bison: Monarch of the Plains* (Portland, OR, 1998)

Frank, Roberta, 'The Invention of the Viking Horned Helmet',
    *International Scandinavian and Medieval Studies in Memory of Gerd
    Wolfgang Weber*, XII (2000)

Gimbutas, Marija, *The Language of the Goddess* (London, 1989)

Gomara, Francisco Lopez de, *La Historia General de las Indias*
    (Saragossa, 1553; Antwerp, 1554)

Haines, Francis, *The Buffalo: The Story of American Bison and their
    Hunters from Prehistoric Times to the Present* (New York, 1970)

Haverstock, Mary Sayre, *An American Bestiary* (New York, 1979)

Hawkes, Clarence, *King of the Thundering Herd: The Biography of an
    American Bison* (London, 1924)

Hornaday, William Temple, *The Extermination of the American Bison*
    (Washington, DC, 2002)

Hussowski, Mikolaj, *Carmen de statura, feritate ac venatione bisontis*
    ('A Song about the Appearance, Savagery and Hunting of the
    Bison') (Kraków, 1523)

Isenberg, Andrew C., *The Destruction of the Bison: An Environmental
    History, 1750–1920* (Cambridge, 2001)

Jonstonus, Johannes, *Historiae Naturalis* (Amsterdam, 1657)

Krasinska, Malgorzata, *Hybridisation of the European Bison and
    Domestic Cattle* (Poland, 1976)

—, *European Bison: The Nature Monograph* (Berlin, 2013)

Krasinski, Z. A., 'The Border Where the Bison Roam', *Natural History*,
    6 (June 1990), pp. 62–3

Leason, P. A., 'A New View of the Western European Group of
    Quaternary Cave Art', *Proceedings of the Prehistoric Society*, vol. V,
    part 1 (1939), pp. 51–60

Lott, Dale F., *American Bison: A Natural History* (Los Angeles, CA,
    2003)

McDonald, J., *North American Bison: Their Classification and Evolution*
    (Los Angeles, CA, 1981)

McHugh, Tom, *The Time of the Buffalo: The Evolution and Natural
    History of The American Bison* (New York, 1972)

Mair, Charles, *The American Bison: Its Habits, Method Of Capture And Economic Use In The Northwest: With Reference To Its Threatened Extinction And Possible Preservation* (Montreal, 1891)

Malotki, Ekkehart and Henry Wallace, 'Columbian Mammoth Petroglyphs from the San Juan River Near Bluff, Utah, United States', *Rock Art Research*, XXVIII/ 2 (2001), pp. 143–52

Mannix, Daniel P., *Those About to Die* (New York, 1958)

Mitchell, Chalmers, P., *Centenary History of the Zoological Society of London* (London, 1929)

Mosionier, Beatrice, *Spirit of the White Bison* (Winnipeg, 1989)

Partington, Charles F., ed., *The British Cyclopaedia of Natural History* (London, 1835)

Patent, Dorothy Hinshaw, *Buffalo: The American Bison Today* (Newton Abbot, 1993)

Paxson, Edgar William, *E. S. Paxson, Frontier Artist* (Boulder, CO, 1984)

Pliny, *The Historie of the World: commonly called, the Naturall Historie of C. Plinius Secondus*, trans. Philemon Holland (London, 1635)

Popper, Deborah Epstein, and Frank J. Popper, 'The Great Plains: From Dust to Dust', *Planning* (December 1987)

Porter, Valerie, *Cattle: A Handbook to the Breeds of the World* (London, 1991)

Pucek, Zdzislaw, 'History of the European Bison and Problems of its Protection and Management', in *Global Trends in Wildlife Management*, ed. B. Bobek, K. Perzanowski and W. Regelin, Transaction of the 18th IUGB Congress (Krakow, 1987), pp. 19–30

—, ed., *European Bison (Bison Bonasus): Current State of the Species and Strategy for Its Conservation* (IUCN, Switzerland, 2003)

Robbins, Ken, *Thunder on the Plains: The Story of the American Buffalo* (New York, 2001)

Roe, Frank Gilbert, *The North American Buffalo: A Critical Study of the Species in its Wild State* (Toronto, 1970)

Rorabacher, John A., *The American Buffalo in Transition: Historical and Economic Survey of the Bison in America* (St Cloud, MN, 1971)

Simoons, Frederick J., *A Ceremonial Ox of India* (Madison, WI, 1968)

Topsel, Edward, *The History of Four-footed Beasts and Serpents* (London, 1658)

Toynbee, J.M.C., *Animals in Roman Life and Art* (London, 1973)

Whitney, Caspar, *On Snow-shoes to the Barren Grounds: Twenty-eight Hundred Miles after Musk-Oxen and Wood-Bison* (New York, 1896)

—, *Musk-Ox, Bison, Sheep, and Goat* (New York, 1904)

White, T. H., *The Book of Beasts* (London, 1954)

Winn, Carol A., *Buffalo Jones: The Man Who Saved America's Bison* (2000)

Associations and Websites

THE AMERICAN BISON SOCIETY

www.americanbisonsocietyonline.org

Formed in 1905 to save the bison from extinction, campaigning to create bison reserves and to stock them with animals bred in zoos. In 1907 a small herd was transported to the Wichita Mountains Wildlife Refuge in Oklahoma. A few years later wild herds were also established in Montana and South Dakota. Once these herds had established themselves the Bison Society disbanded their organization. In 2005 the ABS was relaunched by the American Wildlife Conservation Society to ensure that the now much larger herds were properly monitored and protected.

EUROPEAN BISON CONSERVATION CENTER

www.bison-ebcc.eu

Their main goal is to coordinate the process of the genetic variability maintenance of the species, and to create a platform of communication between European bison breeders, decision makers, conservationists and other interested parties.

BISON SPECIALIST GROUP — EUROPE

ebac.sggw.pl

Advises on technical and scientific aspects of bison conservation in Europe.

LARGE HERBIVORE NETWORK
www.lhnet.org

THE SOCIETY FOR THE PROTECTION OF THE EUROPEAN BISON
Founded in 1922 by scientists to conserve and repopulate the then
almost extinct European bison, or wisent. The Society reintroduced
wisents from zoo collections into the Białowieża Forest in Poland,
where they still exist as a vulnerable species.

INTERTRIBAL BISON COOPERATIVE
www.intertribalbison.org
Has a membership of 56 tribes in nineteen u.s. states with a collective
herd of over 15,000 bison. It was created to re-establish bison herds
on Indian lands. The ultimate goal is to ensure that each tribal herd
will become a successful and self-sufficient operation.

THE NORTH AMERICAN BISON COOPERATIVE
Formed in 1993 and located in the Great Plains of North Dakota,
NABC is a 330-member cooperative of ranchers from the u.s. and
Canada, producing and processing bison meat under the
TenderBison® brand.

MINNESOTA BUFFALO ASSOCIATION
mnbison.org
This non-profit organization established in 1993 is dedicated to
promoting the American bison and its many uses / products. Their
concerns include raising bison in an ethical manner and preserving
the animal as a historic and remarkable American species.

NATIONAL BISON ASSOCIATION
www.bisoncentral.com
In 1995 the American Bison Association and the National Buffalo
Association merged to become the NBA, a non-profit organization of
producers, processors and enthusiasts. The NBA promotes bison
production as a sustainable ranching / farming model and feeds the

consumer's growing appreciation for the great taste and nutritional benefits of bison meat.

Other U.S. commercial organizations primarily concerned with the promotion of bison products in an 'ethical manner' and with a resolve to 'preserve the great American bison as an icon of American heritage' include the Kansas Buffalo Association, Dakota Territory Buffalo Association, Eastern Bison Association, Missouri Bison Association, Iowa Bison Association and the Rocky Mountain Buffalo Association.

Photo Acknowledgements

The author and publishers wish to express their thanks to the below sources of illustrative material and/or permission to reproduce it.

From Ulysse Aldrovandi et al., *Quadrupedum omnium bisulcorum historia* . . . (Bologna, 1642): p. 46 (foot); author's photograph: p. 172; Bodleian Library, Oxford: p. 45 (foot); from (A. E. Brehm), *Der kleine Brehm* . . . (Berlin, 1927): p. 169; British Museum, London (photo © Trustees of the British Museum): p. 100 (foot); photo Buffalo Bill Historical Centre, Cody, Wyoming: p. 139; Buffalo Bill Historical Centre, Cody, Wyoming (Whitney Gallery of Western Art Collection, gift of Mr and Mrs Ernest J. Goppert, Sr, in memory of Mary Jester Allen): p. 107; photo and reproduction courtesy the Buffalo Collection, Scottsdale, AZ – www.buffalo collection.com: p. 95; from Mark Catesby, *The Natural History of Carolina, Florida, and the Bahama Islands* . . ., vol. II (London, 1743): p. 48; from N. H. Darton, *Geologic Atlas of the United States – Syracuse-Lakin Folio Kansas* (Washington, DC, 1920): p. 144; photo Amy Davis/*Baltimore Sun*: p. 137; photo Denver Museum of Nature and Science: p. 131; photo Larry Detmers, reproduced by permission of Peggy Detmers Studio: p. 110; photo Erdélyi Bölény/National Geographic Society/Corbis: p. 51; photo *Fairbanks Daily News-Miner*: p. 130 (top); Francisco Lopez de Gómara, *La Historia General de las Indias* . . . (Antwerp, 1554): p. 45 (top); photo Carol M. Highsmith: pp. 114, 115 (top); from Johannes Jonstonus, *Historiæ naturalis de quadrupedibus libri* . . . (Amsterdam, 1657): p. 47; Kunstmuseum Basel: p. 112; photo The George F. Landegger Collection of District of Columbia Photographs in Carol M. Highsmith's America,

Readers are free:

- to share – to copy, distribute and transmit these images alone
- to remix – to adapt these images alone

Under the following conditions:

- attribution – readers must attribute either image in the manner specified by the author or licensor (but not in any way that suggests that these parties endorse them or their use of the work).
- share alike – If readers alter, transform, or build upon this image, they may distribute the resulting work only under the same or similar license to this one.

Index